Thinking Like
Mathematicians

Thinking Like Mathematicians

*Putting the K–4 NCTM
Standards into Practice*

THOMAS E. ROWAN
BARBARA BOURNE

HEINEMANN
Portsmouth, NH

Heinemann
A division of Reed Elsevier Inc.
361 Hanover Street   Portsmouth, NH 03801-3912
Offices and agents throughout the world
Copyright © 1994 by Thomas E. Rowan and Barbara Bourne

We would like to thank the children and parents who have given their permission to include material in this book. Every effort has been made to contact the copyright holders for permission to reprint borrowed material where necessary. We regret any oversights that may have occurred and would be happy to rectify them in future printings of this work.

Editor: Toby Gordon
Production: Renée Le Verrier
Cover Design: Darci Mehall

Library of Congress Cataloging-in-Publication Data
Rowan, Thomas E.
    Thinking like mathematicians : implementing the K–4 curriculum and evaluation standards / Thomas E. Rowan, Barbara Bourne.
        p.   cm.
    Includes bibliographical references.
    ISBN 0-435-08343-0
    1. Mathematics—Study and teaching (Elementary)   I. Bourne, Barbara.   II. Title.
QA135.5.R72   1994
372.7—dc20   93-43901
                                                   CIP

Printed in the United States of America on acid-free paper
97   96   95   94   2   3   4   5   6   7

Contents

Acknowledgments

The authors wish to thank the children, parents, teachers, and other school system staff who have given their permission and support to the publication of this book. In particular, teachers Chris Oberdorf, Maura Backenstoe, Jill Hudson, and Patty Hughes allowed classroom observations. Patty Hughes, Chris Perretti, Leona Arthur, and Jill Hudson allowed photographs to be taken in their classrooms. The photographer for the Montgomery County Public Schools, William Mills, took all of the excellent photographs.

Project IMPACT, on which the book is based, was supported, in part, by the National Science Foundation. The opinions expressed are those of the authors and are not necessarily those of the National Science Foundation. We are most grateful for the support of the Project IMPACT staff.

We also thank the Montgomery County Public Schools for permitting us to observe and report on Project IMPACT in its early stages of implementation. The school system has been continually supportive of efforts to deliver high quality mathematics instruction to all students.

Finally, we want to thank Toby Gordon and the staff at Heinemann for their excellent assistance and support while the book was being developed and published.

MATH POWER

*A*nne *Ikeda asked her kindergarten students how they could determine the number of **single** mittens that would be needed for every student in the class to have one pair of mittens.*

After providing time for each child to work with a partner, Ms. Ikeda brought the children back together to share their ideas with the class.

Rosa was among the first to offer a plan of action. "I'm going to go around and tap everybody on the head and count," she said. Her teacher nodded. "Then I'm going to go around and do it again."

"Why will you go around a second time, Rosa?" asked Ms. Ikeda.

*"Well, because everyone has **two** hands!"*

* * * * * * *

Tyrone, a first grader, was handed seven sticks of ten unifix cubes, a pencil, and a sheet of paper with the problem

$$68 - 50 = \square$$

Tyrone ignored the unifix cubes and, after only a few moments of thought, wrote the number 18 in the box.

"How did you do that, Tyrone? What was your thinking?" the teacher asked.

*"Well, I thought 50 plus 50 . . . ," began Tyrone, then stopped and thought. "No, no," he continued, "I thought 50 **minus** 50. That's 0. Then I said, that means that there's 10 more to get to 60, and then 8 more to get to 68. The answer is 18."*

Rosa and Tyrone are thinking like mathematicians. They are not intimidated by math, nor are they overly concerned about hearing the teacher say that their answers are correct. Each is confident, creative, and actively involved in the math process. In fact, at this early point in time, Rosa and Tyrone are well on the road to realizing their "math power."

Math power. Another trendy phrase? More educational jargon? Not to those who work with Rosa and Tyrone, for despite the children's obvious high-level thinking skills, success in math *could* be out of their reach. Each attends an elementary school on the outskirts of a large city where, as in many similar schools, the standardized test scores are usually quite low. Typically, the odds are against high academic achievement in urban neighborhoods with low income and inadequate resources. However, Rosa and Tyrone could beat the odds because empowering children in mathematics has become an increasingly important component in both children's schools.

Rosa's and Tyrone's teachers are rethinking their teaching strategies and math curriculums to align more closely with the basic goals of the National Council of Teachers of Mathematics' (NCTM) *Curriculum and Evaluation Standards for School Mathematics.* The NCTM *Standards,* which recommends fundamental revisions to current mathematics instruction, has set five basic student goals:

1. learning to value mathematics
2. becoming confident in their ability to do mathematics
3. becoming mathematical problem solvers
4. learning to communicate mathematically
5. learning to reason mathematically (pp. 5–6).

The NCTM *Standards* emphasizes the need to provide children with opportunities to construct, for themselves, a solid mathematical foundation. This view arises at least partly from the assumption that an understanding of children's intellectual, social, and emotional development should drive the primary-grade curriculum. Children need to continually interact with their environment, constructing, modifying, and integrating ideas. Placing students in carefully planned situations provides opportunities that extend natural modes of learning to benefit mathematical ends.

In classrooms that focus on the goals of the NCTM *Standards,* children like Rosa and Tyrone are encouraged to build their math power. They do not sit passively, listening to a teacher who controls the way they do math, nor do they watch quietly while a few highly verbal children dominate class discussions. They spend little time memorizing arithmetical algorithms and rules that they don't understand. Instead, these students are provided with multiple situations that build, and build on, their mathematical backgrounds and personal interests. Students in these classrooms are allowed to solve problems in ways that are meaningful to them: they work cooperatively with their peers; use a variety of manipulatives; receive guidance through insightful teacher questioning; and have ample time and opportunity for thought, reflection, and discourse. Consequently, the children see themselves as doers of mathematics—as mathematicians.

These classrooms are rarely quiet, but instead hum with the sounds of small voices sharing experiences and ideas. As children work in small groups, they are able to collaborate on shared activity—explaining, debating, defending, negotiating, evaluating, and eventually concurring—in a collegial atmosphere. Large group meetings provide forums to air alternative solutions. Teachers regularly ask, "Did anyone do this a different way?" until each unique method is unearthed. In listening to classmates explain how they arrived at an answer, students learn to value the thinking of their peers and quickly discover that there is no one correct way to "do math."

Because their teachers value *thinking* more than *answers,* these students are increasingly willing to persist, participate, and share. They can be certain that every idea will be treated with respect and that they will be allowed to complete their explanation without interruption. Students' processes and solutions are rarely wrong, although some may address questions other than the one currently under investigation. In fact, these children often discover errors for themselves when allowed the time and freedom to explain and explore their answers.

Teachers are discovering that the benefits of this type of program are not confined to mathematics alone. As active participants in the process of math, students incorporate the expressive and receptive components of communication—listening, speaking, reading, and writing—thereby augmenting and enhancing their basic language skills. In these math environments, children think, talk, write, and even model or draw out their mathematics expressions. At the same time, they must actively attend to the ideas of others in order to debate and negotiate shared solutions.

The interaction of mathematics and language has proven beneficial to other content areas as well. The same kind of thinking that is recommended by the *Standards*—to understand, to communicate, and

Children in classrooms that implement the NCTM Standards have many opportunities to make sense of mathematics.

utilize mathematics—also serves as a powerful tool for interpreting information, visualizing concepts, and implementing solutions in subjects such as social studies, science, and art.

Classrooms that take the NCTM *Standards* seriously empower students by enabling them to feel that they are in control of mathematics rather than that the mathematics is in control of them. Problem-solving tasks, move from traditional textbook-driven, formulaic problems, to encounters with real-life situations that inspire creative solutions. Children instinctively see the value of mathematics as they make connections between it and the real world. They begin to reason mathematically and communicate their ideas through the language of math. Most importantly, because they are constructing their own knowledge, children become confident in their ability to meet the challenge. They are mathematicians.

2
· · · · · ·
DIRECTIONS FOR CHANGE:
THE NCTM *STANDARDS*

One episode of the comic strip "Calvin and Hobbes" suggests that math is like a religion because you have to accept its ideas and results on faith. "No one can say how it happens," Calvin explains. "You either believe it or you don't."

Unfortunately, many students share Calvin's philosophy. They view mathematics as a set of unfathomable rules to memorize, be tested on, and eventually forget. Many adults instill in children the belief that only the "whiz kids," the "Einsteins," have the innate ability to understand the logic and processes of mathematics.

You don't have to look too far beyond the Sunday comics to see the need for a change in attitude towards mathematics. The crisis in American schools is well documented. Test scores appear low, and many people feel that students in the United States compare poorly with their counterparts around the world. Business leaders report that American workers are often ill prepared to meet the demands of the workplace and many adults wonder whether students will be ready for the advanced technological nature of the society into which they will graduate. Indeed, it is difficult to go through a week, or even a day, without encountering references to the crisis in American schools, most specifically in mathematics and science education.

In the early 1980s, several national reports alerted parents and educators to an impending educational crisis. Reports such as *A Nation at Risk* (1983) and *Educating Americans for the Twenty-First Century* (1983) documented many of the problems facing our schools and established the need for reform.

Americans were further alarmed when international achievement results indicated that many of our students perform less successfully in mathematics than students educated in other countries, many of which are less wealthy and less technologically advanced than the United States. In comparison to students from other nations that participated in the testing, Americans scored about average on computation skills, those skills that require memorization and direct application of rules and algorithms.

The greatest disparities in achievement between American students and those from higher-scoring nations appeared to be in the areas of critical thinking—problem solving and mathematical reasoning. (Tests given entirely within the United States confirm the imbalance favoring skills and computation. This has been interpreted by some to indicate relatively poor performance overall.) Such test results, coupled with the decline of American competitiveness in the world economy and the increased importance of technology, led scientific and educational leaders in the United States to call for drastic action to improve the teaching of science and mathematics.

In 1986, the NCTM responded to the challenge by appointing the Commission on Standards for School Mathematics to create a vision of mathematical literacy and develop a set of national standards to guide schools towards that vision. The resulting document has been the most significant response yet to the call to improve mathematics teaching and learning. (This first document has been followed by a second, *Professional Standards for Teaching Mathematics* [1991], and a third is being developed to provide standards for math assessment.)

Production of the *Standards* proved a rigorous and time-consuming process, but the NCTM was committed to a product that would truly meet the educational needs of all students and teachers. A team of twenty-six mathematics educators was chosen from the United States and Canada to represent a wide spectrum of the educational scene. Its members included public and private school teachers, college educators, supervisors, and researchers, representing all levels of mathematics education from elementary through graduate school.

After one year's intensive work, a preliminary draft was completed and distributed nationally. The audience was diverse—students, teachers, parents, scientists, and mathematicians, as well as politicians and leaders from business and industry. After another year, which included careful review of the respondents' input, the writing committee revised its final document. The NCTM's *Curriculum and Evaluation Standards for School Mathematics* was released in March of 1989. The nation now had a set of standards with which to prepare its students for the twenty-first century.

DO WE NEED NATIONAL STANDARDS?

National standards—the very concept raises questions for American parents and educators who have grown up believing in the autonomy of independent school districts. What exactly are national standards? Are they really necessary or is this just an excuse for more educational mandates; a different set of rules and regulations; a national test that must be "taught to"? And just what is the difference between national standards and a national curriculum?

In his April 26, 1992, "Message from the President," of the National Education Association (NEA), President Keith Geiger referred to national educational standards as "statements of quality" directing school improvement. The term *national standards,* he said, does not imply developing a national curriculum—or national test. Unlike a curriculum, which spells out content scope and sequence and specific learning outcomes, standards are broad, far-reaching goals that establish a direction in which education should point.

True to this definition, the NCTM *Standards* is indeed broad in scope. Rather than isolating and prescribing specific content grade by grade, the report uses a four-section format, dividing the recommendations among three broad age groups, grades K–4, 5–8, and 9–12, and then devoting an entire section to evaluation standards.

The NCTM commission was concerned with identifying basic math concepts and attitudes that need to be fostered in all children, but the foundation for its recommendations was its knowledge of and commitment to how children learn and, more specifically, how they learn mathematics.

DIRECTIONS OF CHANGE

While the need for change is only too obvious, some may find the commission's recommended means of change a radical departure from a time-honored system. Many would agree, however, that the *Standards* sets out a plan that is exciting, challenging, and clearly committed to children and their individual growth in mathematics.

Schools committed to incorporating the *Standards* may need to rethink many long-established modes of classroom operation. To this end, the NCTM commission provides a clear direction for change, calling for the elimination of some deeply ensconced classroom routines. Rote memorization of "math facts" must be replaced with strategies for deriving those facts and conceptual understanding of math processes. The teaching of established algorithms should give way to exploration of and respect for individualized methods of finding answers. Pencils and paper must have their place beside manipulative materials, calculators, and everyday objects in classrooms.

For some, these new ideas will be a drastic change from established classroom procedures, a step into a whole new sphere of teaching practice. Others will recognize familiar themes that they already incorporate into their classroom programs. But most will find common ground—a collective starting point—in the five basic goals set forth in the introduction of the *Standards*. As mentioned in Chapter 1, these goals expect students to value mathematics, be confident in their own abilities, be mathematical problem solvers, and communicate and reason mathematically.

The *Standards* never recommends omitting specific informational knowledge from the mathematics curriculum. Instead, it suggests a reevaluation of mathematics processes, procedures, and emphases in the classroom. The following powerful statement can guide the nature of mathematics instruction.

> "Knowing" mathematics is "doing" mathematics. A person gathers, discovers, or creates knowledge in the course of some activity having a purpose. This active process is different from mastering concepts and procedures. We do not assert that informational knowledge has no value, only that its value lies in the extent to which it is useful in the course of some purposeful activity. (NCTM *Standards,* p. 7)

THE K–4 STANDARDS

In addressing the specific needs of primary-grade children, the K–4 *Standards* makes several important assertions about children and how they can best achieve the characteristics described in the five goals—characteristics that define children as young mathematicians.

1. The understandings that children already have when they enter school should be valued and built upon. Children enter school with the ingredients essential to budding mathematicians—a variety of life experiences from which they can draw context for learning, a well-developed vocabulary (although it may not be English), some rudimentary mathematical concepts and skills, and best of all, a highly tuned sense of curiosity. When mathematics programs begin with these strengths, newly acquired concepts take root easily and form a system that is sufficiently strong to support additional learning.

2. The K–4 curriculum should be developmentally appropriate. A developmentally appropriate curriculum recognizes that young children are naturally social, active, and curious and need to explore new ideas in safe, enjoyable, and stimulating environments. They require ample time to develop their own meaningful procedures, and often must revisit new concepts several times in a variety of contexts. Children need to be physically involved with materials, and they need opportunities to reflect upon and then discuss their actions. This process facilitates their transition from concrete and literal perceptions of their world to abstract ideas and generalizations.

3. The quality of content and instruction is far more important than the quantity. The goal of the math program should be to build understanding rather than to have students memorize many rules that may or may not be understood or remembered. This requires that children have sufficient time to inquire, explore, discuss, and revisit ideas so that they can build deep conceptual meaning.

4. Children should build confidence in themselves as mathematics learners. To accomplish this, the instruction must be designed to ensure success for all students. A multimodal approach helps teachers address all learning styles. Children need opportunities to create their own methods of problem solving and the assurance that their teachers and peers will value their thinking as creative and viable.

5. Children must be actively involved in doing mathematics. They must interact with the physical world and with other children and supportive adults. Concrete materials are essential to provide the foundation for children just developing the ability to think abstractly. Hands-on activity is critical to "doing" mathematics, and the basic language components—speaking, listening, reading, and writing—serve as necessary links between action and mathematical understanding.

6. Children should see how mathematics is applied in other subjects and in daily activities. Children will value mathematics as an essential life tool when they see it incorporated throughout the curriculum. Mathematics helps to make meaning out of other content areas, specifically science and social studies. However, its application should not be restricted to academic disciplines. Classrooms offering strong mathematical programs will apply concepts through incidental daily routines and activities.

7. A broad range of content should be taught. Programs that emphasize computational skills over other mathematically related areas present an imbalanced mathematics curriculum. Math can be fun and interesting to students for it is far more than memorized facts, rules, and procedures. Children need to apply mathematical concepts as they explore, develop, test, and describe ideas that help them make sense of their world, and they need to see that mathematics is one way to understand, describe, and communicate about the world in which they live.

8. Calculators and computers should be used appropriately as both computational and instructional tools. Calculators and computers can complement mathematics instruction and enhance understanding. Besides assisting computational efficiency, they provide a means for students to investigate patterns and algorithms in ways that would be impossible otherwise. Classroom technology adds a dimension to the instructional program that could not be achieved with pencil and paper alone.

What a radical departure this list is from traditional assumptions about learners and their environments! These assumptions focus on the nature of the students and the interaction of the students with the mathematics, rather than on some artificial analysis of traditional content. They incorporate documented research about the growth and development of young children in determining what to teach and how to teach it. They recognize that real mathematics is dynamic and process oriented, rather than static and answer oriented.

The following is content shown within the photograph:

December

Days	Sunny	Cloudy	Partly Cloudy	Rainy	Snowy
16					
15					
14					
13					
12					
11					
10					
9					
8					
7					
6					
5					
4					
3					
2					
1					

The season is _winter_. Today is _Thursday_, _January_ _14_, _1993_.

Yesterday was _Wednesday_ _January 13_ _199_... Tomorro... ...riday

January _1_... ...93...

weather is cl...

Sat.
Saturday
2

The NCTM Standards *advocates incorporating mathematics into many daily activities.*

Classrooms that adopt these premises will be active places where teachers pay constant attention to how well the children are making sense of the mathematics being studied. To facilitate this process, programs will incorporate what the children have experienced outside of the school setting so that new ideas can be learned with understanding, and they will allow children to construct their own mathematics knowledge through such activities.

The NCTM *Standards* is not simply theory and rhetoric. To help teachers achieve both the content and the spirit of the document, the *Standards* provides background information and examples of appropriate mathematics activities. These are organized under thirteen specific standards for grades K–4, which can be used to evaluate existing curricula and/or develop new curricula.

1. Mathematics as Problem Solving
2. Mathematics as Communication
3. Mathematics as Reasoning
4. Mathematical Connections
5. Estimation
6. Number Sense and Numeration
7. Concepts of Whole Number Operations
8. Whole Number Computation
9. Geometry and Spatial Sense
10. Measurement
11. Statistics and Probability
12. Fractions and Decimals
13. Patterns and Relationships

The first four standards represent broad avenues for empowering children in mathematics. Standards five through thirteen designate specific mathematics concepts to be addressed in the classroom. Accompanying all of them are discussions and suggested activities to help teachers accomplish the intended outcomes.

PUTTING THE *STANDARDS* INTO PRACTICE

When implementing the *Standards,* teachers are encouraged to incorporate several distinct elements into the mathematics program. They informally assess student progress throughout the day and take care to value each child's learning style and individual approach to math problems, no matter how far from the traditional path it may wind. Teachers

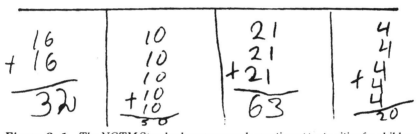

When I measured with links, I noticed that...

2 desks was 32 links,
5 arms was 50 links,
3 chair was 63 links
and 5 desks openings is
20 links. 3 desks was 48.

$$
\begin{array}{c}
16 \\
+\ 16 \\
\hline
32
\end{array}
\qquad
\begin{array}{c}
10 \\
10 \\
10 \\
+\ 10 \\
\underline{10} \\
50
\end{array}
\qquad
\begin{array}{c}
21 \\
21 \\
+\ 21 \\
\hline
63
\end{array}
\qquad
\begin{array}{c}
4 \\
4 \\
4 \\
+\ 4 \\
\underline{4} \\
20
\end{array}
$$

Figure 2–1   *The NCTM* Standards *recommends creating opportunities for children to interact with their environments, and connect their experiences with mathematics concepts.*

can provide opportunities for children to solve problems in meaningful situations; use manipulative materials; work cooperatively with others in small groups; develop their own procedures to solve math problems; talk about the mathematics they are using; and encounter math throughout their curriculum—in language and reading, social studies and science, art, and physical education.

Activities that are developmentally appropriate reflect children's need to actively interact with their physical and social environments in order to develop intellectually, socially, and emotionally (see Figure 2–1). Hands-on experiences and those activities that appeal to children's natural curiosity tap a sense of inquiry in children and serve to stimulate discovery and mathematics learning.

But hands-on activity, in and of itself, is not enough. Children must make connections—connecting their classroom experiences with prior experiences, and connecting these with mathematics concepts. Communication activities, discussions with classmates and teachers, and writing about math experiences help students make these connections. Without such discourse, the hands-on process may actually become an alternate procedure that bears no real relationship to the mathematics or a child's prior experience.

The NCTM *Standards* recommends that teachers utilize mathematics throughout the school day, as well as foster its incorporation into take-home activities. A good way to help children see how mathematics is applied in other subjects and in the real world is to call attention to these applications across the curriculum. These need not, and should not, be restricted to academic content areas. Daily routines such as recording attendance, calendar activity, and assigning classroom chores are rife with mathematics potential.

Most children arrive at school with the tools necessary for success—curiosity, communication skills, and a variety of life experiences. Upon entering school, young children are able to solve problems that call for computational skills they have not yet learned. However, after several years of traditional mathematics instruction, they become less creative and rely on memorized procedures. The result: their problem solving skills and performance actually drop (Carpenter and Moser, 1984). This is consistent with the results of the international test scores in which American students performed better in computational skills than in problem solving and mathematical reasoning.

Mathematics programs that implement the NCTM *Standards* encourage teachers to provide children with opportunities to share experiences from outside the school and connect those with the mathematics that is being learned within the school. This does not happen automatically. Children must be encouraged and given time to relate school mathematics to their personal experience through personal reflection, student-student, and student-teacher discussions.

Children in the United States have the same intellectual capacities as any other children around the world; there is no reason to believe that any geographic area or ethnic culture has a corner on innate mathematical ability. As classrooms adopt techniques that encourage students to retain and apply the skills with which they enter school and construct their own mathematical procedures, our students will be better prepared to serve as productive members of the global community.

3

......

CHILDREN CONSTRUCTING KNOWLEDGE

*T*he raucous sound of irate chicks almost drowned out the voice of first-grade teacher Chris Valentine as she gathered twenty-three children around her. Eight posters, labeled Squeaker, Chirp-Chirp, Peep, Feathers, Stripey, Chicago Jackson, Alex, Jr., and Kate, hung beside her chair, displaying data the students were keeping on their noisy classroom pets. The chicks were now nine days old and ready for their second weigh-in, but the children were told that before they updated their chick's statistics, they should estimate what they thought the weight would be.

Nicole collected Feathers, her data sheet, a pan balance, and a box of unifix cubes to use as units of measurement. Her friend Tanya came over to help her get started.

First they estimated. Taking note of the fact that just six days earlier Feathers had weighed nine cubes, Nicole estimated that her chick would now weigh ten cubes. But Tanya, commenting on how big Feathers had grown, estimated thirteen cubes.

Feathers was deftly placed in a deep plastic tub on one side of the pan balance scale and an identical tub was counterbalanced on the other side to hold the unifix cubes. The girls began their work. Nicole counted aloud as Tanya dropped cubes into the tub by twos. "Two . . . four . . . six . . . eight . . . now put in two more . . . ten," directed Nicole. The scale did not shift. "Maybe it has to be thirteen," said Nicole, conceding that perhaps Tanya's estimate was right. "Put in three more." The pan still did not balance. Nicole and Tanya exchanged looks of surprise. "Maybe get three more."

Tanya left to join another group, so Nicole continued alone. She began adding more cubes to the tub, one or two at a time, but did not count aloud. Finally, Feathers' tub began to rise. Nicole added just one more cube and Feathers' tub rose higher than the tub of cubes. Nicole reached in and removed several cubes, slowly replacing them one at a time until, once again, Feathers' tub sat too high.

Nicole reached in and removed one red cube. Feathers' tub sank slightly below the other and Nicole immediately replaced the cube, returning the tub to its higher position. She carefully pulled out a green cube, with the same result. She repeated this action several more times, each time being careful to remove a different color cube and then returning it to the tub. But the pans never balanced. Finally, she shrugged her shoulders and counted the cubes in the tub.

"How many cubes?" asked Ms. Valentine.

"Twenty-three," she replied, "but I don't believe it."

"Why not?"

"She [Feathers] was only nine [Feathers' previous weight]. That's too much."

A boy from the next table stopped by to ask how much Feathers weighed, "Twenty-three." said Nicole. "It's too many."

He looked quizzically at Nicole. "The other ones are only like twenty-one," he said and returned to his own chick.

Nicole decided to weigh Feathers again, quickly dropping cubes into the bucket. This time she wasted little time trying to get the scale to balance, stopping when the pans sat almost level. Removing cubes by twos, she counted them into a pile.

"How many did you get this time?" asked her teacher.

"Twenty-three."

"Do you believe it?"

"Yeah, okay, I believe it," she said with a shrug and recorded the number next to her original estimate.

It was, indeed, hard to believe. Feathers had been the smallest chick at birth, and weighed a mere nine cubes when three days old. As the weights of her siblings were recorded and posted, word spread through the class that, at twenty-three cubes, Feathers was now the heaviest of the lot.

Nicole is experiencing math. She is acting on objects and noticing their relationships. She observes, tests, and retests. She uses her intuition and background knowledge to develop hypotheses, devise plans, draw conclusions. She communicates ideas. In essence, Nicole is constructing her own mathematical knowledge.

Children are curious by nature. They are born problem solvers. From the earliest age, they delight in their interactions with the world around them, handling, manipulating, experimenting. Most importantly, they take note of the physical changes and social responses brought on by their actions. And with each new encounter, they modify their perceptions of the world and begin to construct their own knowledge of the elements within their environment.

Similarly, a child's ability to learn the abstract processes and concepts integral to mathematics benefits from the opportunity to interact directly with the environment. As children manipulate objects, observe changes, develop trial-and-error methods of interaction, and reflect upon their experiences, they gradually construct their own understanding of the relationships between objects and concepts. By placing children in controlled, problem-solving situations and providing a supportive environment to communicate ideas, teachers can build effective learning opportunities.

Traditional approaches to mathematics usually focus on rote learning and prescribed algorithms. All students are expected to work towards the same objective, at the same time, in the same manner. Lessons are conducted by teachers who transmit a single method of computation through direct instruction. Students are expected to absorb this method, commit it to memory, and recall it whenever it is needed. The focus is on a product—a correct answer.

The approach recommended by the NCTM *Standards* on the other hand, begins with the assumption that students must construct for themselves personal understandings of mathematics concepts and processes. Each student is seen as a unique individual who, given a meaningful situation in the proper setting, is able to wrestle with a problem and devise a workable solution. The focus is on the process—building an understanding that can be transferred to other situations.

CONSTRUCTING MEANINGS

Nicole and the other first graders in Ms. Valentine's class are used to tackling meaningful math problems. This time it was real chicks, real scales, real units of weight, and real jobs—reading, estimating, measuring, recording, and comparing. The task could have been accomplished more quickly and efficiently as a demonstration by Ms. Valentine, perhaps with a few students in front of the class, but as Ms. Valentine realizes, constructing knowledge is not a vicarious process.

Feathers weighed twenty-three cubes (or, as Nicole came close to discovering, twenty-two and one-half cubes). But the weight of any one chick on a given day was not what was significant about the exercise. What was significant that day were the *processes* involved in discovering Feathers' weight and the relationship among the various elements of the lesson.

Closer analysis of Nicole at work shows a child actively involved in learning. Nicole's simple counting reveals a rudimentary understanding of addition. She added cubes by twos until she had reached her estimate of ten cubes. "Two, four, six, eight . . . put in two more . . . ten," she said as her friend dropped cubes in by twos. "Put in three more," she added so they'd reach Tanya's estimate of thirteen. Without realizing it, she was using the basic concept of missing addend subtraction.

When the scale failed to balance, Nicole became concerned with the weight of the individual cubes. She was determined to balance the scale, and when adding and removing single cubes did not help the pans balance, she decided to focus on their one apparent difference—color. Soon she discovered that this attribute was insignificant to her task. The second time Nicole weighed the chick, she ignored color differences, and quickly decided for herself when the tubs were "close enough," a concept basic to measurement.

Nicole's original hypothesis, that Feathers would weigh only ten cubes, fell far short of Feathers' actual weight. Just how far short was hard to believe. Seeing that pile of twenty-three cubes in the tub hardly convinced her, and when she heard that the other chicks were weighing in lighter than little Feathers, she decided she'd better repeat the process.

This very sophisticated move for a first grader indicated her grasp of the multiple elements involved in the chicks as a group, and Feathers' assumed place within that group. The numbers did not make sense to her, so she repeated the process, this time more quickly and efficiently than the first. The results were the same, the evidence was hard to dispute. Twenty-three cubes. "Yeah, okay, I believe it," she conceded, and in the group discussion that followed, it was obvious that the others did as well.

Would Nicole have believed Feathers' weight if she had not been so actively involved in the process? Perhaps. But more important was the confidence and autonomy she exhibited in developing a process of measurement and evaluation. She made an initial prediction that reflected earlier findings. She tested several methods to get the pans of the scale level, but rather than abandoning the project when she failed to achieve the desired balance, decided for herself when the balance was "close enough." She knew when to question her results, and had enough confidence in herself to retest an answer that seemed unacceptable. Finally, she was able to accept that evidence as plausible and move on to the second phase of the day's lesson.

After all the groups had recorded their data and rehung their posters, the children reassembled around their teacher. It was time to discuss what they had discovered about the weights of their chicks. Ms. Valentine began by posing several questions, to which students actively responded. "Who estimated their chick's weight correctly?" "If you didn't estimate correctly, was your estimate more than or less than what your chick weighed?" "Which chick weighs the most?" "What did you notice about Feathers?"

After the group had talked about her questions, Ms. Valentine opened the discussion to student-initiated comment, allowing the children the freedom to discuss their own ideas about the chicks. Together, they analyzed the data, comparing the weights of the chicks.

Soon Ms. Valentine sent the students back to their seats. "Put everything away except for your unifix cubes," she instructed them. "And look towards the overhead."

The children quickly cleared their desks and turned towards the overhead screen. "Now, we know that Peep weighs twenty-one cubes and Chirp-Chirp weighs twenty cubes," Ms. Valentine began. "If we put Peep and Chirp-Chirp together on a scale, how much would they weigh?" She wrote the addition problem on the overhead

$$\begin{array}{r} 21 \\ + 20 \\ \hline \end{array}$$

and told the children they could use cubes or any other props they needed to help them find a solution.

The hum of activity began immediately as Ms. Valentine moved about the room. Several children sat back confidently, explaining to Ms. Valentine how they had mentally computed the problem. Others worked singly or in pairs, using their unifix cubes to work out the answer. After about five minutes, Ms. Valentine returned to the front of the class and called on students to share their methods.

Nicole and Tanya had worked together with the unifix cubes. They quickly went to the overhead and began arranging transparent tiles to represent the cubes. "Tanya is making twenty-one and I'm making twenty," explained Nicole as they strung out two long lines of cubes. "We each got our number," continued Tanya. "This is Chirp-Chirp," she said, pointing to the line of twenty squares. "And this is Peep." She pointed to the line of twenty-one. "We know that 20 and 20 is 40 and we added one more."

"Danielle, you used the cubes but you grouped them differently," said Ms. Valentine beckoning Danielle to the front of the class. "Watch how Danielle groups them." Danielle began to set her tiles in double sets of five.

Soon Danielle was ready to explain her method, but as she pointed to each row of five, she recited, "ten . . . twenty . . . thirty." She stopped, noticing something was wrong. Slowly, she began to remove some tiles. She appeared confused.

Ms. Valentine told her to take a few minutes to figure out what she'd done, and used the time to let the children who'd used mental math share their reasoning. "I knew that 2 plus 2 was 4. I knew that 1 plus 0 was 1," began Albert. "So it just makes 41 because two 10s and two 10s equal 40 and 1 plus 0 equals 1. So it's 41."

By the time several others had shared, Danielle was ready to continue. She had replaced all of the original squares and pointed to the rows of markers as she quickly counted, "five, ten, fifteen, twenty, twenty-five, thirty, thirty-five, forty and one is forty-one."

MAKING CONNECTIONS

Hands-on activity takes on new meaning when the hands are needed to gently move, measure, and manage a squawking, flapping chick. Ms. Valentine's first graders directly experienced the physical attributes of shape, weight, and balance while collecting their data. The activity itself provided the motivation to learn, and the fact that Nicole and her classmates could discover something totally unexpected significantly enhanced the thrill of discovery. But understanding is not built solely by experience. Experience and discovery must be accompanied by children *making connections* between previously internalized concepts and newly developed interpretations of the world.

The activity of weighing chicks set the stage for discussion and was essential to the work that followed. The discussion then allowed the children to take ownership of their experience by giving structure and meaning to arbitrary numbers and new concepts. Combining the weights of Peep and Chirp-Chirp provided a logical reason to add double-digit numbers and gave significance to the numerals. The children knew what they were adding, for they had each handled and counted twenty or twenty-one blocks just minutes before.

Using manipulatives helps young children make sense of abstract ideas and processes.

Prior to this lesson, Ms. Valentine's class had had multiple experiences with place value and double-digit addition and the children were well prepared to solve this problem. Even so, the children showed a full range of sophistication in their various solutions. Many children tackled the numbers quickly, without the aid of any manipulatives; but those who were not ready to perform the addition mentally had the time and props to establish a solution, and a partner with whom they could share the task and co-invent a plan of action.

VALUABLE DISCOURSE

The lesson culminated when the children explained their solutions to their classmates. Albert quickly and easily verbalized the procedure he used to add the two numbers. Nicole and Tanya jointly shared the responsibility for explaining a method in which they assigned a row of cubes to represent each chick's weight. Danielle, who had used an elaborate grouping procedure, started her explanation easily enough, but soon got tangled up explaining her more complicated method. Ms. Valentine wisely allowed Danielle the time she needed to think through her work and she was soon able to explain her steps in a logical manner.

Verbalizing a thought process focuses ideas for a student. It organizes thinking. It solidifies concepts and processes and establishes them as a basis for future reference. And it provides ownership of ideas.

Often, children solve a problem intuitively and are unable to state how or why they gave a particular answer. The initial solution may have come to them in such a flash of insight that they did not even see their own procedure. It is only when they explain how they arrived at a solution that they actually develop and establish their procedure and build processes to use and modify when faced with similar problems.

When children explain their thinking, they have the opportunity to decide for themselves whether or not they are correct. The process of explanation enables them to revisit their thinking and say, "Yes, I'm right. I've explained it, I know this makes sense. I've confirmed what I thought." If their response is incorrect, or the process they used to arrive at their response is flawed, they can stop themselves and say, "This is not making sense, let me retrace my steps and decide where I went wrong. Then I can figure this out."

Ms. Valentine's class is a terrific example of students gaining math power. Knowing that each child must actively construct his own knowledge, this skilled teacher has provided the students with meaningful situations and then allowed them the opportunity to reflect on their experiences and thought processes. Discourse is integral to her curriculum—children are provided with multiple opportunities to share, debate, explain, and evaluate their ideas in small and large group settings.

It is interesting to note that Ms. Valentine's class is very diverse. Some children have been identified by the school system as "gifted and talented," and a significant number receive Chapter One assistance. A range of culture and ethnicity is represented in the classroom. Yet every child participates in and benefits from the math lessons.

Letting children construct their own knowledge allows teachers to reach the full range of students. Traditional methods of direct instruction, while appearing to work for some, fails to work for a large percentage of students. Those who benefit little from traditional approaches include children from all achievement groups—from average students to those in special education; both those considered "slow learners" and those labeled "gifted and talented."

All children are unique. They enter learning situations with different backgrounds. They exhibit distinctive learning styles. They develop in their own way, and at their own pace. Consequently, each child will interpret and connect ideas differently and must construct for himself or herself the connections and relationships among those concepts essential to understanding mathematics.

4
......

TEACHERS AS PROBLEM SOLVERS

Sue Evans, a first-grade teacher, is committed to allowing her students to construct their own mathematical understanding. She admits, though, that even after participating for two years in a program designed to help teachers understand and use the kinds of ideas found in the NCTM *Standards,* she still must fight the urge to intervene. She likes to recount one classroom experience that illustrates how children can be trusted to solve complex problems for themselves when provided with meaningful situations—sometimes going far beyond typical first-grade problems.

"We were doing fractions and I was having the kids dividing different objects into parts with masking tape," she relates. "The children got to choose the object they wanted to divide and then draw a number from a pile. This number told them how many parts they were to create. One group of three average-achieving girls chose to divide the 'cubbies,' an area of thirty-two separate boxes stacked sixteen on top of sixteen. The number they drew was six.

"One-sixth of thirty-two! Well that was one of my most difficult problems of the day, certainly more difficult than any I'd envisioned when planning this activity. When I saw the task ahead of them I thought, 'They'll never be able to do this.' But they wanted to try. So I went over to them and started asking a series of questions, trying to sway them to do it my way. But they wouldn't hear of it, saying 'No, no, we've got our own ideas,' so I went on to other children.

"From time to time I would look over towards the cubbies and notice that things looked confused. They had tape all over. When it came to their turn to talk about what they'd done, I thought, 'I'll skip them, maybe they won't notice.' But no, they had to explain. I thought, 'Oh these poor girls, they're not going to be able to explain this.'

"Then one of the girls said, 'One-sixth of thirty-two cubbies is five and one-third.' All I could say was, 'WHAT?' and she said it again. 'One-sixth of thirty-two cubbies is five and one-third.' And I said, 'Can you explain that?'

"The girls explained how they took the cubbies and divided them into six parts and they had five cubbies in each part. They had two cubbies left over, so they took those two cubbies and divided each one into thirds, so that would be six. Then they went back and counted and it was five and one-third.

"Well, I was just shocked with what they were doing! If you wrote on a piece of paper one-sixth of thirty-two, it would seem an impossible task for first graders. But the cubbies were there, they had the tape, they could count, they could change it around."

Certainly, the performance of these first graders would surprise most adults, and indeed, few children in traditional classrooms would be able to solve a problem such as one-sixth of thirty-two. But given real-world situations, ones in which they are truly interested, children often attempt, and realize, fantastic results.

Research (see, for example, Whiten, et al., 1990 and Carpenter and Moser, 1984) suggests that children enter school able to solve real problems that require mathematics skills they have not yet been taught. But sadly, by the time they reach second grade, many of these same students exhibit a decrease in their creative abilities.

Why is there a deterioration in problem-solving success? One explanation appears to be an emphasis on "teaching" mathematics algorithms, facts and rules, rather than letting young children construct their own understanding. This leaves children little to fall back on when faced with new situations.

Problem solving in the real world is not based on memorized performance. It requires thinking. Like the girls in Ms. Evans' class, children need to tackle problems with confidence, understanding, creativity, and perseverance.

One second grader who was known as a "math whiz" became lost when he moved on to the third grade. The source of his confusion? The second-grade teacher had told her students that when adding double-digit numbers, they should always start on the side by the piano. The child interpreted this as a rule to be followed, but unfortunately for him, the piano was on the other side of the classroom when he got to third grade. While this scenario demonstrates an extreme misuse of "rules," is it that far removed from having children learn "borrowing" and "carrying" without understanding place value, or having them rely on "clue words" embedded in a story problem to decide on a course of action?

What then, can teachers do to create an atmosphere that encourages growth, rather than loss, of mathematical thinking skills? Like Sue Evans, many approach the teaching of mathematics with the same tenacity and creativity with which they wish their students to approach the task of learning mathematics. They view the teaching of mathematics as a problem-solving activity in and of itself—an effort to find situations and problems for children that will enable them to make sense of the mathematical aspects of the world in which they live and work.

Teachers are responsible for controlling the classroom setting. To incorporate the NCTM *Standards,* they must present problems and provide situations that enable students to construct their own understanding of the math. They need to build on these situations by asking questions and guiding discussions so that their students will construct understanding while staying close to the main mathematics goals of the curriculum.

An essential role of the teacher, then, is to find situations that will be meaningful or interesting to children and develop math content from these situations. Conversely, she must also take mathematically relevant concepts and create interesting learning experiences that will make these concepts meaningful to students. This is a teacher's problem to solve. Teachers can call upon a variety of sources for ideas, including personal experience, school district instructional guides, documents such as the NCTM *Standards,* and the textbook and its teachers' guide.

Children need to be put in problem situations that lead them to develop their own ideas and understandings through direct experience and discourse. In day-to-day classroom situations, a variety of ways exist to encourage and support students as they develop their mathematical understanding. Sometimes, a teacher can direct children towards the intended outcome through careful questioning or guided class discussion. At other times, it may be necessary for the teacher to establish a stronger foundation of more rudimentary concepts.

Ms. Marina Lopez's second graders had been working on double-digit subtraction for some time and she felt they were ready to deal with a problem that required regrouping. She wrote the problem "63–56" on the board. The children made several attempts to solve the problem, but soon acted frustrated. Some had subtracted the smaller digit from the larger one. Others had tried to start with the tens and didn't know what to do next. And some had actually determined the correct answer, but did not realize it or understand how they got it. It wasn't long before many of the children declared, "That's too hard. We don't know how."

Since it was close to the end of the class, Ms. Lopez debated what to do. Certainly, one of her options was to show the traditional procedure for getting an answer; but after a moment's thought, Ms. Lopez decided not to continue. "Okay," she said to the children, "if you think it's too hard, let's think about it some more and we'll come back to it another time."

That night, Ms. Lopez went home and thought about real-world situations that would lead her students to solve the problem. Knowing that the children had been busy planning a student-operated "Fun Fair," she seized on an authentic situation for them to work out.

The next morning Ms. Lopez reminded her students that in listing the supplies they would need to operate all their games, they had determined they needed a total of twenty-four beanbags. Good news, she continued. She had come across sixteen beanbags in the school storage closet. How many more beanbags, she asked, would they need? Vitally interested in the answer, the children found the it quickly and fairly easily.

"How did you solve this?" she asked.

"I knew that 6 plus 8 is 14," said one, "and 16 plus 8 must be 24. So the answer had to be 8."

"I used my fingers to count 17, 18, 19, 20, 21, 22, 23, 24," said another as she tapped each finger in turn. "Then I counted the fingers."

"I subtracted 16 from 24," said another child, who had paper and pencil in hand. She went on to explain her subtraction with regrouping procedure—just the direction in which Ms. Lopez had been trying to move the class.

Discussing the various problem-solving methods—addition with a missing addend, counting on, and subtraction—the class began to notice the similarities among the different procedures. As the discussion proceeded, Ms. Lopez recorded some of the procedures in symbols. She then brought back the subtraction problem from the previous day. The children were able to attack the problem with new confidence and solved it with little difficulty. Soon, they were ready to discuss how to record what they had done and to solve similar problems in the same manner.

Ms. Lopez saw the need for the children to establish stronger connections between concrete experience and a computational exercise presented in symbols. But it took flexibility and self-confidence on her part to stop her planned lesson when she saw her students were not ready. There is a fine balance between the needs of children and the demands of a curriculum or textbook. Feeling the pressure to move through the curriculum as scheduled, many teachers might not have chosen to invest the extra time in what seems a simple subtraction process.

The need to construct strong mathematical foundations for children is too important to warrant pushing them ahead merely for the sake of completing a unit, and teachers like Ms. Lopez feel that time spent ensuring that students fully understand the rudimentary concepts is never wasted. Although such an approach seems to consume more time initially than the "demonstration and practice" approach, any additional time spent in the early stages of learning will be rewarded later. Students who construct their own procedures are much better positioned to transfer their knowledge to new circumstances, everyday problems, and the mathematics concepts they will study in the future. And teachers are likely to find that the need for reteaching is minimized.

The ultimate goal, then, must not be to "get through" the lesson, the unit, or the year. Rather, the goal must be to construct a solid foundation so today's children can get through the more complex problems that will come later. To this end, a long-term teaching plan, whether teacher-developed or based on a text, should be used with flexibility, insight, understanding, and continual reevaluation.

As teachers place themselves in the role of problem solver and seek solutions that will help children build a clearer understanding of mathematics, they can develop effective classroom instructional programs for mathematics. For those who believe that children should be constructing their own knowledge, the focus must be on valuing the mathematics process.

One way to approach the process of *teaching* mathematics is to view it as analogous to the process of *doing* mathematics. Even in the most challenging situations, mathematicians often follow a simple, four-step problem-solving process. The plan, which allows them to understand, compute, and revise (if necessary), enables them to solve most problems they encounter. The plan requires that they

1. understand the problem
2. develop a plan that they feel will solve the problem
3. try the plan to see if it works
4. look at the results to see if they make sense for that problem. If the results do not make sense, they move back to the first step of the process and begin again.

In teaching, a similar four-step process can be used. In this process teachers must first understand the mathematics that is to be taught and the children who are learning the mathematics. The second step is to develop a plan that reflects that understanding. The third step is to provide classroom instruction that implements the plan. And the fourth step is to evaluate students' success, reflect back and possibly revise the approach.

This is one method of establishing classroom practices that respects child development, ensures the application of sound educational principles, and accommodates for the needs of individual classrooms, teachers, and children. Certainly, there is no single strategy that will work in every classroom. However, those classrooms in which teachers incorporate this process and develop instructional programs that reflect the recommendations found in the NCTM *Standards* will share many of the following characteristics:

- They will focus on the process of mathematics, rather than on right answers.
- They will encourage students to describe their thinking verbally and in writing.
- They will enable students to value mathematics as a useful and interesting area of learning.
- They will encourage students to be less reliant on the teacher and better able to validate their own answers as correct.
- They will encourage students to be persistent and willing to seek alternative ways to solve problems that are not solved on the first attempt.
- They will show and model mathematical ideas in a variety of ways. This will include multicultural uses of mathematics as well as hands-on experiences that use various manipulatives.
- They will enable children to become problem solvers and users of mathematics in their everyday lives.
- They will develop an efficient and encompassing program of mathematics instruction.

5

BUILDING UNDERSTANDING

*M*artin Lee, the teacher's assistant for the kindergarten, asked Sara to count for him. She happily and confidently complied, counting to 35 with no hesitation. Then Mr. Lee showed Sara seventeen dried beans. "Count these for me, Sara, and tell me how many there are."

Sara smiled broadly and counted away, "one, two, three . . ." However, she had no way of keeping track of which beans had been counted. Some beans were counted several times, others not at all. After a while, Sara announced, "Twenty-four." She was done.

Mr. Lee was beginning to understand Sara's level of mathematics understanding. Based on his knowledge of general child development theory, he may not have been surprised by Sara's inability to transfer her rote counting skills to a one-to-one correspondence with real objects.

Many kindergartners are able to rote count when they come to school. This does not mean that they understand what they are doing, even though they have given a "right" answer. When teachers understand at what level the child is performing, they can make decisions about an appropriate mathematics program.

In this case, Mr. Lee knew that kindergarten children should begin to demonstrate an understanding of the counting process. This means that they can keep track of their count, count each object only once, assign only one number to each object, and associate the number that ends the count with the number of objects in the group. Children like Sara, who despite their ability to rote count cannot make such connections, need experiences that will develop these concepts. Advancing Sara too quickly, based only on her counting skills, would be a mistake.

Children need many math experiences to help them develop number and operation sense.

BUILDING UNDERSTANDING

The best mathematics programs are built on three types of understanding—understanding how children learn; understanding the mathematics itself; and understanding the background, needs, and abilities of each student.

UNDERSTANDING HOW CHILDREN LEARN

Learning is an active process. From their first year, children interact with their physical and social environments to build a framework of knowledge, a mental organization which then becomes the foundation for making sense of future events. New situations and perceptions are assimilated into this existing scheme of knowledge, but often they do not fit into the child's current notions about the world. Consequently, the child must modify and adapt what she already knows to accommodate this new information. In this way, the child constructs new knowledge and understanding to meet future encounters. Through assimilation and accommodation, children are continually constructing knowledge. They are learning.

The ability of young children to reason abstractly is limited; learning must be directly linked to personal actions and physical objects. As they pass through the early stages of childhood, children are increasingly able to apply representational language and symbols to objects and ideas. Moving into the primary grades—kindergarten through grade three— children's modes of reasoning expand and more complex thought processes emerge, broadening the opportunities for learning. But even for the most mature students, mental activity still must be well grounded in concrete experiences.

Like Sara, most children like to listen and imitate, and because of their increasing vocabulary and their ability to remember and repeat what they have heard, it is easy to overestimate what children in the early grades actually know and understand. Being sensitive to the stages at which children can apply representational language and symbols to ideas, understanding the development of their reasoning ability, and realizing the link between concrete experience and abstract thought are fundamental to mathematics instruction.

To understand concepts, to truly *learn,* a child must be confronted with problems that are challenging—problems that cannot be solved by routine repetition of previously learned procedures. Such problems will be most valued by the student when they are presented in meaningful situations that relate to the child's background. This provides a "hook" to associate new experiences with old, so that preexisting notions can be modified and conceptual understanding constructed.

While more mature learners can represent objects mentally, for most young children, reasoning and perceptions are limited to direct personal experience; they require physical action and manipulation of objects. Obviously, the greater the variety of activities and the wider the assortment of materials, the richer will be their learning experiences and the stronger their foundation of understanding. However, it must be noted that learning experiences are not solely comprised of physical activity. The adaptation of mental structure necessary for learning to take place requires adequate opportunity to reflect on an event.

Somewhat paradoxically, independent construction of knowledge is often facilitated by social interaction. Children need to reflect on their physical actions to build understanding; but verbalizing their ideas helps them to organize their thoughts and reorder their thinking. Exchanging mathematical notions with classmates and adults helps to clarify problems, provides insight into alternative solution strategies, and identifies potential conflicts or misconceptions. Communicating so that other students understand a solution requires a child to focus on descriptions, define procedures, and rationalize conclusions. Conversely, listening to others provides new perceptions and encourages students to further modify and reorganize their own ideas.

Arleen Cohen-Hart likes to provide many opportunities for her third graders to explain their thinking. One of the class' favorites is a mental math game in which students must quickly choose a problem, solve it mentally, and then explain how they arrived at their solution (see Figure 5–1). By offering a range of difficulty, Ms. Cohen-Hart accommodates the mathematical range of the students; by limiting the number of displayed problems, she ensures that each problem will be explained several ways. Ms. Cohen-Hart notes that almost every time she uses this activity, the students' reactions indicate that they have heard strategies that they would not have thought of on their own and that they are anxious to try.

UNDERSTANDING THE MATHEMATICS

Before teachers can plan or implement a program that reflects the *Standards,* they should understand what "knowledge of mathematics" means and have some level of comfort with the many concepts integral

Figure 5–1
MENTAL MATH ACTIVITY

Overview
Have children do arithmetic mentally and explain their thinking.

Level
Adaptable

Grouping
Total class or small group

Materials
- Overhead projector
- Transparencies with five to ten addition, subtraction, or a mix of the two kinds of problems on each.

     A wide range of difficulty helps ensure that each student will be able to participate in the activity. A sample set of problems for third grade:

2 + 2 + 2	2 + 2 + 3 + 3	2 + 2 + 2 + 10
40 − 20	40 − 21	40 − 19
14 + 3	14 + 13	14 + 18

Procedure
- Have students pair up with partners.
- Before turning on the overhead, tell students that when they see the problems on the screen, they are to choose two or three problems and work them out in their heads.
- Suggest the possibility of choosing two or three problems from the same line if they relate to one another (as they do in this sample).
- Ask students to be ready to share their answers with their partners and be able to explain how they arrived at their solution.
- Turn on the overhead projector. Have students signal when they are ready to share.
- When all students have signaled that they are ready, have partners share their answers and solutions with each other.
- Have students come together as a class. Each time a child shares a solution and method of deriving that solution, ask if anyone did that example in a different way. Discuss different methods for finding solutions.

Extensions
- During whole group discussion, have students try to explain their partner's approach if it was different from theirs.
- Have student pairs make up their own problems for the activity. For each problem they create, they should write out at least one method for solving it.

to mathematics. Then they need to understand how to present these concepts in a developmentally appropriate manner.

This does not mean that every elementary teacher must be a mathematician. It means that teachers must recognize mathematics not as a static collection of right answers, but as a dynamic activity in which people (including children) make personal sense out of quantities, shapes, sizes, and patterns.

Children learn through observation and social interaction with the external world. Because understanding mathematics also requires that specific observed relationships be generalized and represented symbolically, mathematical understanding is built by reasoning, which is an internal process.

Observable characteristics, such as size, weight, color, and shape, provide knowledge about physical attributes. Words and names provide a common nomenclature with which to communicate. A child building with a set of blocks soon discovers their physical properties: edges and corners keep blocks from rolling, larger blocks balance better at the bottom than at the top of a stack, and blocks hurt when they land on a toe. The terms *rectangle, tower,* and *heavy* provide the social context with which the child can communicate about her blocks and her discoveries. But it is an understanding about the relationships among and numerical ideas about the blocks that provides the framework for mathematics. Which ones are bigger? Are there more red blocks than blue? How many more? How many different ways can these blocks be categorized?

Early mathematics knowledge is directly linked to physical knowledge. To see relationships, children must observe the nature of things. Such knowledge cannot be built without adequate opportunities to observe and act on objects; without sufficient time to reflect on the consequences of those actions; and without ample opportunity to communicate about these observations. Inherent in any good mathematics program are opportunities for children to construct relationships and make sense of numbers through classifying, comparing, ordering, counting, measuring, and patterning, along with opportunities to reconstruct their actions through reflection and discourse.

Upon careful examination, many seemingly simple mathematical concepts reveal multiple layers of complexity. Concepts that do not appear difficult on the surface may hold subtle challenges for teachers of young children. Keeping in mind both the nature of the child and the nature of the math concept can alert teachers to potential instructional difficulties.

One common example of a complex mathematics concept is that of fractions. Ms. Evans, the teacher discussed in Chapter 4 whose first-grade fraction unit includes many hands-on activities, is aware of the problems students can encounter when learning about fractions. She knows that at its most basic level, the concept of a fraction is relatively simple for a child to grasp; naming two equal parts as halves is not difficult. However, extending this rudimentary concept to a generalized understanding of fractions, especially one that incorporates the use of fraction *symbols,* is much more difficult.

Ms. Evans is familiar with the concepts integral to fractions and is prepared for the misconceptions and difficulties in generalizing that her students may develop along the way. Young children often struggle with the illogical characteristics of fractions, not the least of which is the seemingly absurd notion that the value of a fraction decreases if the value of its denominator increases.

A child in first (or even second) grade is often still grappling with the symbolic representations of whole numbers. The number 1 represents one of something, 2 represents two. Next she learns that sometimes a 1 and a 2 are placed side by side to form a different number, 12. It may be difficult for the child who does not yet fully understand this combination to now accept that a 1 and a 2 written vertically with a small line between them is something else altogether, one-half. Sometimes the symbol is even written horizontally with a slanted line between the 1 and the 2.

Generalization of the fraction *concept* is more difficult than understanding the symbol. "One-half" is easy when it is encountered in context, such as dividing an apple into two equal pieces for a snack. But extending that idea to one-third, one-fourth, one-fifth, and then to the idea that the denominator tells how many parts the whole is divided into and the numerator tells how many of the parts are used, is indeed difficult for most children. To further complicate the issue, the "whole" to which the denominator is applied can represent either a single object or an entire collection of objects.

Like Ms. Evans, teachers who have a basic understanding of both the mathematics concepts and how children approach those concepts are prepared with developmentally appropriate, yet mathematically logical, instructional approaches. Many decide it is better to delay the

Young children, especially those who encounter fraction symbols in the early grades, need a variety of hands-on experiences to help them develop the part-whole concept.

introduction of fraction symbols until the children have a good enough understanding of the symbolization of place value, which probably doesn't occur until the upper elementary grades.

Unfortunately, as desirable as it may be, delaying fraction symbols is usually overridden by local curricula, texts, or standardized tests. But Ms. Evans and her colleagues do their best to maintain a hands-on approach by regularly incorporating spoken or written fraction words into their discussions—"one-half of the class," "three-fourths of the orange." Their students are provided frequent, comprehensive, hands-on experiences, either in real-world situations or through the use of manipulative materials, to develop the part-whole concept. Furthermore, these teachers take into account the fact that such experiences are especially critical when the "whole" represents a collection of things rather than a single object.

The importance of understanding the mathematics is not confined to overtly complex concepts like fractions. Even seemingly simple concepts such as those that underlie whole numbers can be complicated. For example, many children have difficulty understanding place value, but by being alert to the children's level of understanding and then using many hands-on activities and opportunities to share and discuss their activity, teachers can help them construct this concept for themselves.

This became clear to Arleen Cohen-Hart and her colleagues when they decided to conduct one-on-one mathematics interviews with the first-, second-, and third-grade students in their school. They discovered that, although the students were able to identify and compute with double-digit numbers, many of the children did not truly understand place value.

In the assessment, each student was given a series of tasks involving the number 17. First the student was asked to read it, then to count out that many chips. Virtually all the children performed these tasks with ease.

Then the teacher pointed to the numeral. Circling the 7 with her finger, she said, "Use these chips to show me how many this part of the numeral means." The near universal response in all three grades was correct—seven chips. Next, the teacher circled the 1 and said, "Now show me with the chips how many this part of the numeral means." Almost every first grader, a majority of the second graders, and many third graders responded by showing a single chip. Even after a follow-up query ("Yes it is a one, but does it mean anything different in *this* numeral?"), most of the children still said it meant just one chip. These students needed continuing opportunities to help them construct their understanding of place value.

Sometimes it helps when teachers put themselves in the place of the child. At an elementary math workshop, Ms. Cohen-Hart shared a video of Miko, a second-grade student who was having difficulty regrouping. Miko was asked to solve the problem $45 + 17 =$ ____. She rewrote the problem in vertical form and promptly wrote a 1 above the 4 in the tens column. Then she stopped. Asked by Ms. Cohen-Hart what she was thinking, Miko responded, "I know that $5 + 7$ is 12 and that I have to 'carry the 1' over here (she pointed to the tens column), but I don't know what to do with the 11 I have left." When asked where she had heard the word 'carry,' Miko explained that her father had told her. Ms. Cohen-Hart now realized that Miko was being frustrated by rules for which she had no understanding.

The teachers agreed that Miko's lack of understanding indicated she was not ready to learn and use traditional algorithms for computation *with understanding*. They discussed how teachers who are aware of the complexities of place value and the common math misconceptions among young children are better able to recognize potential pitfalls and then plan appropriate instructional strategies. Such teachers encourage children to interrelate their work with materials and symbols for as long as necessary so that they can fully develop the concept that the 1 in the tens place means one ten and not just one. When this does not happen, children like Miko resort to the magic of memorized algorithms: "carry the one over here," or "knock on the door in the tens column and borrow a one." But such dependence on rote memorization of rules can prove devastating in the later mathematical development of these children.

The teachers then went on to do an activity themselves, using base-ten blocks to solve the same addition problem. First, they were asked to show 45. All of them did so by grouping four "longs," each of which represented ten units, and five ones. Then they were asked to use another set of blocks to show 17. Once again, each used one long to represent the 10 and seven ones to represent the 7. Finally, they were asked to combine the blocks to find out how much this was altogether.

Nearly every teacher pushed the longs (tens) together first, and then combined the ones, so each had five longs and twelve ones. The majority then exchanged ten of the single units for another long (representing ten units), yielding six longs and two ones. Others just left the ones and counted them in that form (see Figures 5–2, 5–3, and 5–4).

After completing the hands-on activity, the teachers were handed paper and a pencil and were asked to make a step-by-step numerical record of what they did. They found this somewhat awkward since they were well-versed in the traditional pencil-and-paper algorithm, but all agreed it was not truly difficult to combine the tens first, then the ones, even with pencil and paper.

Given blocks, the child who has not fully developed her understanding of ten as a unit would approach the same problem in what she considers to be a perfectly normal way, combining the tens first, then the ones, and then regrouping or exchanging ten of the ones for another single ten. When the teacher tells her she must follow a different procedure— add the ones first, then regroup, and finally add the tens—before she understands the process, what is she to do? She might rely on tricks she does not understand, but as in the case of Miko, this may not help her find a solution.

Lucky for Miko, she is in a class like Ms. Cohen-Hart's, where the teacher recognizes the subtleties in the mathematics content, and where

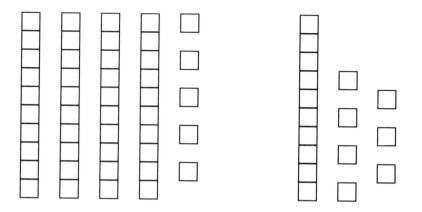

Figure 5–2   *45 is 4 longs and 5 ones. 17 is 1 long and 7 ones.*

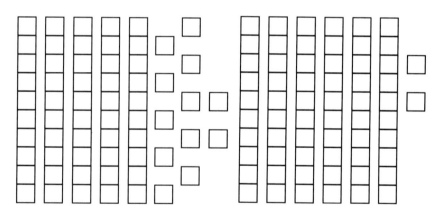

Figure 5–3   *Combine to 5 tens and 12 ones.*

Figure 5–4   *Exchange 10 of the ones for 1 long. 6 tens and 2 ones is 62.*

THINKING LIKE MATHEMATICIANS

43

children like Miko are provided enough time and hands-on experience to construct their own understanding of ideas.

Children should not be made to feel that their right ideas are wrong just because they are not traditional. Ms. Cohen-Hart worries, however, that her students will be burdened with inefficient, nontraditional methods. To test this, she and the others in her workshop group tried the base-ten block experiment again, this time using three- and then four-digit numbers. It wasn't long before they decided that few children would want to continue doing a pencil-and-paper computation starting in the largest-valued place once they understood place value. They would move to a more efficient procedure. Over the years, Ms. Cohen-Hart has observed that when given a chance, most children reach the same conclusion on their own, without being made to feel dependent on rote memorization.

UNDERSTANDING THE BACKGROUND, NEEDS, AND ABILITIES OF EACH STUDENT

Before a teacher can set up meaningful situations in which her students can build mathematics knowledge, she must first understand the individual backgrounds of her students.

Children enter school from a wide variety of situations. Many arrive at school fortified with an assortment of enriching experiences. They may have spent several years in a quality preschool setting, or at home with a caregiver who nurtured their language development and fostered their innate curiosity with books, trips, and a variety of experiences. Other children come from settings that are culturally different or that offered them few physical and social advantages. These children often arrive at school less prepared to meet the challenges of a conventional, English-speaking kindergarten program. But while their observable and testable skills might make them appear less developed than others in the class, these children simply have had a different, and less traditional set of experiences. In a child-centered classroom, nontraditional experiences can prove to be mathematically meaningful when seen and used appropriately. To do this, teachers must collect as much student information from as many sources as possible.

For children beyond kindergarten, school records and conversations with the previous year's teachers provide a variety of specific student data. Checking out the personal backgrounds of students helps teachers choose meaningful teaching strategies. It is important to know what the primary language of the children and the children's families is, and to be aware of any unusual home situations and the diversity of family structures. A school-based student profile may include standardized test scores, but anecdotal records and student portfolios present a better picture of student behavior and physical and cognitive capabilities, as well as academic achievement. Simply knowing the previous teacher's classroom strategies can help teachers determine how well children are prepared for the planned instructional program.

Although school records provide details and information, many teachers choose to assess the students for themselves. Children mature over the summer, gain specific knowledge without the help of organized instruction, and respond differently in different classroom settings. It does students a disservice to form expectations—especially negative ones—based on records or conversation alone. Engaging students in a variety of interesting activities during the first several weeks of the school year allows a teacher multiple opportunities to assess current language, math, reading, and writing skills, as well as to observe their general physical and social development.

In some schools, teachers conduct informal telephone conversations with parents early in the year to establish a line of communication with them as well as obtain background information that is valuable for planning classroom instruction. In addition, they often follow up with a letter to parents at home. The letter introduces the teacher and explains her mathematics program (see Figure 5–5 on page 46).

In schools where many parents have difficulty reading or writing in English, teachers can replace the letter with a personal conversation, perhaps using volunteers who speak the language. Children from homes where English is not the primary language are often at a higher risk of failure in our school system. Knowing the backgrounds of these students allows teachers to include instructional approaches that encourage each student to talk about family and societal traditions.

Valuing the cultural diversity of the children allows the mathematics to contribute to a positive social atmosphere, and teachers in any school can incorporate a multicultural component into their curriculum. Instruction that appeals only to the customs of the majority culture puts many students at a disadvantage and deprives all students of enriching opportunities. Not only does a multicultural program broaden every child's cultural awareness and understanding, it provides even more opportunities to see mathematical ideas in different settings.

Figure 5–5

Dear Parent/Guardian of _____ :

    As _____ 's kindergarten teacher, I want to welcome you to our school family. I am looking forward to an exciting and rewarding year in which my students will learn many new things. In mathematics we will be studying beginning uses of numbers, shapes that are around us, what it means to measure things, patterns, addition and subtraction concepts, and many other exciting ideas.

    I want to do everything I can to make sure that your child has a successful and pleasant year. You can help. Regularly talk to your child about school. Make your conversation friendly and informal. Ask questions that allow your child to openly describe the day's events.

    If there is anything that you feel would be helpful for me to know as I work with your child, I would appreciate hearing from you. By working together, we can ensure your child has the best possible year.

    If you have any questions now or at any time this year, please be sure to give me a call at 555–1111. I look forward to hearing from you.

    Thank you for your help,

_____
(teacher's signature)

Those who teach in schools with diverse student backgrounds, know firsthand that they must accommodate for the linguistic components of mathematics. Language structure and syntax are not universal and can cause confusion in understanding.

Several of Allen Morton's second-grade students were counting coin values. Six children stood at the front of the room holding cards that showed three nickels and four pennies. Emilio, a child of Hispanic heritage, was asked how much money was shown.

"Fifty-four cents," he responded.

Mr. Morton called on another student who responded, "Nineteen cents." The second student was asked to show how he got his answer. He came forward and counted, "Five, ten, fifteen, sixteen, seventeen, eighteen, nineteen."

Mr. Morton then asked Emilio for the amount again. "Fifty-four cents," he responded once more.

The teacher asked Emilio to explain his method and he proceeded to count. "Five, ten, fifty, fifty-one, fifty-two, fifty-three, fifty-four." Mr. Morton could now see that Emilio was confused with the teen numbers. He knew that the English language practice of naming the ones value before the tens value only with the teen numbers is very difficult for many children, especially those from cultures where this is not the practice. The Spanish name for 16 is diez y seis—10 and 6, *with the 10 named first. Emilio's counting process was right on target; he simply needed help understanding the teen numbers.*

Mr. Morton asked the other children to work on a new problem. While they were doing that he asked Emilio to exchange each of the nickels for five pennies, and then count the amount as all pennies. Soon, Emilio was able to exchange the pennies for nickels again, and count out the nineteen cents.

How lucky for Emilio that his teacher took the time to have him explain his thinking, and that Mr. Morton understood both the math content and the cultural factors affecting Emilio's mathematics learning.

6
......

DEVELOPING A PLAN

It is the fortunate teacher, indeed, who finds herself in complete control of her classroom mathematics program. In reality, most public school teachers have the first step in planning handed to them in the form of a textbook or local curriculum. But although it may be true that local mandates dictate the general scope and sequence of the mathematics program, each teacher can, and must, look at the children, the setting, the textbook and/or curriculum, and place these within the context of her knowledge of what is developmentally appropriate for children and conducive to learning.

ONE TEACHER'S PLAN

Pamela Jackson teaches second grade in a large suburban county school district. Teachers there are expected to follow the county's mathematics curriculum and are responsible for their students' mastery of many specific learning outcomes. Ms. Jackson enjoys teaching math and has always devoted at least an hour each day to mathematics instruction.

Until 1991, Ms. Jackson's long-range plans came directly from the county curriculum guide and her daily lessons came from the student texts and workbooks. This left her little room for creativity and little opportunity to individualize instruction for her students. Ms. Jackson's method was traditional: teach, review, test, then reteach if necessary. Like many teachers, she rarely made it through the book before the end of the year. Then, she took part in a special program designed to help teachers understand and use the kinds of ideas found in the NCTM *Standards*.

The program changed forever the way Ms. Jackson views, plans for, and incorporates mathematics into her teaching. She no longer relies solely on textbooks and workbooks. She has added a greater variety of hands-on activities, problem-solving situations, and small- and large-group discussions into her program. There is still a specific "math time" every morning, but children now encounter math concepts throughout the day, from the morning's "early bird" activity to the time the children line up for the afternoon bus that will take them home. As a bonus, not only has Ms. Jackson been able to satisfy all the learning outcomes of her mandated curriculum, she has time left over at the end of the school year to explore new mathematics ideas.

Ms. Jackson is still responsible for teaching all content areas included in the county's second-grade mathematics curriculum, but the focus of her instruction has changed and so, consequently, has her method of planning. No longer does she flip open the curriculum guide to "Unit 1" to see what she will be teaching in early September, and no longer does she feel bound to follow the guide's sequence or timing. In fact, there are units she chooses to omit from her formal teaching plan altogether; she simply incorporates these concepts into her daily routines.

The first thing Ms. Jackson does when planning her math program for the year is to look at the curriculum guide and determine which concepts will require the most time and how she can better develop these concepts through daily activities. In her first years of teaching, Ms. Jackson would plan a unit for graphs, a unit for patterns, one for numeration, one for odd and even numbers, and so on. But now she has found that much of this content can be addressed outside of her long-range planning. She feels that concepts such as numeration, odd and even numbers, and graphing can be presented more efficiently and effectively when they are consistently encountered and revisited on a daily or weekly basis. Other content areas, such as measurement, time, and money can be introduced through incidental daily activities, and then expanded upon in specific, content-based units of instruction. More difficult concepts—place value, regrouping, and fractions—require extensive, well-planned instructional units. In these areas, Ms. Jackson feels, her students need numerous, progressive experiences in order to build the strong foundation necessary for understanding.

For September, Ms. Jackson plans activities designed to familiarize her students with the math routines and concepts they will encounter throughout second grade. They start off the year with lots of informal graphing, patterning, and calendar activities; they use manipulative materials; and they speak the language of math. Ms. Jackson reserves this first month as a time to get to know her students and their abilities. At the same time, her students spend the month gaining confidence as thinkers and doers of mathematics, for indeed, math is everywhere in Ms. Jackson's class.

A quick glance around the room on any given day affords just a hint of the numerous math activities the children will encounter. A large, horizontal bar graph charts the children's favorite pizza. On the same wall hang directions on how to make patterns from names, a large calendar, a weather graph, a money chart, an "odd-even" box, and lots of student-drawn patterns. A number line along the top of the chalk board counts toward the hundreth day of school. One easel displays a page of geometric shapes and equations and another holds a chart explaining how to graph the letters in the week's spelling words.

Ms. Jackson has developed an extensive repertoire of math activities to link her daily plans with the learning outcomes her students must master in second grade. Each morning her students do an "early bird" activity when they enter the class. It may involve spinning a spinner and recording the data, or rolling a cube and recording the numbers that come before and after the number rolled. They also do a "graph of the day," creating and interpreting surveys of interest to them. Over the course of the year, they use bar graphs, line graphs, circle graphs, and Venn diagrams.

Three times a week they do the calendar. "Doing the calendar" in Ms. Jackson's class means more than just naming the day, date, and weather. It is a well-planned, multifaceted activity. Students place the date on the calendar, decide if it is odd or even, and talk about the patterns that emerge with each added number. They may do jumping jacks equal to the date, or handclaps equal to what they think the next day's date will be. "What will the date be on this day?" Ms. Jackson might ask, pointing to an empty square several days away. Or "What day will it be three days from now?" Children write answers on their small clipboards and then discuss with a neighbor how they arrived at their answers. Then the children discuss it as a class. Finally, they decide "how much the day is worth" by arranging various coin combinations to represent the monetary value of the day's date. One child might use a quarter to represent the twenty-fifth of the month while her neighbors use two dimes and a nickel, five nickels, or twenty-five pennies.

Planning ways to introduce these basic concepts in daily activities facilitates long-range planning. For example, in this class, students do a unit on money in January, but by the time January arrives, they have

"Early bird" activities in Ms. Jackson's classroom have children using a variety of materials independently.

DEVELOPING A PLAN

Ms. Jackson posts a new question each day for her students to graph.

had numerous experiences with coins: they recognize the front and back of each coin, they know the names and values, and they have counted coin combinations. Because the children can easily demonstrate the first objectives of the "money curriculum" before the unit even begins, they have ample time to work on the more complex learning outcomes, such as making change from a dollar.

Ms. Jackson has discovered that some content areas, such as graphing, do not require separate units at all. The children more than master the county's basic objectives—creating and interpreting simple bar graphs, picture graphs, and line graphs—as a result of their daily graphing activities or through the mathematics that is integrated into their social studies or science units.

When planning her units of math instruction, Ms. Jackson takes another look at the textbook and her county curriculum guide and evaluates the suggested lessons and how her students will relate to them. Many of the activities she finds are good ones, and she often adapts these to suit the needs of her multicultural class. She then maps out a number of other hands-on and problem-solving activities that will advance the children towards the intended math concept.

Name _Sarah_ ——— Date ———
Think of all the different ways to make a triangle. **Excellent Work**

		Making Triangles with 20 Links			
Triangle	1	6 links (base),	7 links (side),	7 links (side)	side /\ side base = 20
Triangle	2	9 links (base),	5 links (side),	6 links side	side /\ side base = 20
Triangle	3	4 links (base),	8 links (side),	8 links (side)	side /\ side base = 20
Triangle	4	3 links (base),	9 links (side),	8 links (side)	side /\ side base = 20
Triangle	5	2 links (base),	8 links (side),	8 links (side)	side /\ side base = 20
Triangle	6	5 links (base),	6 links (side),	9 links (side)	side /\ side base = 20
Triangle	7	7 links (base),	6 links (side),	7 links (side)	/\ = 20

Great Thinking

On the lines below write 2 things you noticed above.

I noticed that there is a lot of whys to make triangles with only 20 links. My hyest base number is 9. My hyest side number is 9 and my other hyest side number is 9 to.

Figure 6–1 *Ms. Jackson incorporates activities that combine geometry, addition, problem solving, and writing skills.*

As is typical among second-grade classrooms, Ms. Jackson's group represents a wide range of ability and achievement, so she must plan activities to accommodate all students and strive to challenge each at his own level of understanding (see Figure 6–1).

Recently, she had her students writing equations from pattern blocks. The children traced blocks, counted the sides of each block, and then wrote equations that added the total numbers of sides. For example, a triangle (three sides) and a trapezoid (four sides) form the equation $3 + 4 = 7$. The class assignment was simply to choose five sets of pattern blocks and write five corresponding equations.

Even the least advanced students were able to complete the activity. However, many were ready for more demanding work, and Ms. Jackson was able to adapt the lesson to accommodate them. One boy who was particularly ready for a challenge was asked to find as many combinations of blocks as he could that would total twenty-four sides. Doing this forced him to grapple with that number; he had to count by 3s, 4s, and even 6s, which are more difficult tasks than counting by 2s or 5s. He was even able to incorporate some early multiplication skills as he arranged various combinations of triangles, quadrilaterals, and hexagons to total twenty-four sides.

Ms. Jackson finds that planning has become second nature. She can easily determine which concepts her students grasp better in daily experiences and which require extensive time and detailed, focused activity. She doesn't feel rushed, and she no longer has trouble making it through the curriculum before the end of the school year. Best of all, she feels both she and her students are getting more out of the mathematics program by incorporating the principles of the NCTM *Standards*.

ESTABLISHING A PLAN

Each classroom presents a unique blending of student backgrounds and personalities, teacher training and preference, and district curriculum mandates. It would be ideal if teachers fully knew the children before developing a plan for the school year. But as this is rarely the case, it is important that each teacher enters the year with a set of long-range goals and objectives that she would like to have students attain by the time they complete the grade. It is equally important that the teacher be prepared to adapt these goals into daily and weekly plans that reflect the needs of her particular students, enabling them to move successfully towards the desired outcomes.

Whether they have the autonomy to plan or are handed a specific curriculum to follow, teachers have many choices to make. Which concepts need to be taught and which are already known? Which are better taught in formal units and which informally in daily activities? Which concepts are the most critical to these children? Which will be the most difficult and perhaps require the most time? What sequence will best allow the children to build on concepts they already have constructed for themselves? And what milestones should be set in order to reach the goals for the year?

According to the NCTM *Standards,* a primary-grade mathematics curriculum will "build beliefs about what mathematics is, about what it means to know and do mathematics, and about children's views of themselves as mathematics learners (p. 16)." To accomplish these ends, it may be necessary to modify math texts or other prescribed curricula, find connections with other subject areas, and attempt to ground mathematics concepts in a variety of settings.

When setting up a long-range plan it may be helpful to review some of the NCTM *Standard*'s basic assumptions for the K–4 curriculum (pp. 17–19). These can be used as guideposts for choosing content areas, determining specific teaching strategies, and deciding upon meaningful activities.

The K–4 curriculum should be conceptually oriented. Allowing children to build mathematical concepts requires time. When children rote memorize rules or facts with little regard to understanding, their teachers may well believe the children are ready to move quickly through the curriculum. But constructing *understanding* cannot be hurried. Because learning cannot be separated from meaningful experience, it is the development of meaningful experiences that must drive the curriculum plan. The concepts that children build for themselves provide a foundation for new learnings. A memorized rule or fact is quickly forgotten, but understanding has "staying power."

The K–4 curriculum should actively involve children in doing mathematics. If children are to build their mathematics understanding through meaningful experience, they must be doing real mathematics activities. This means using real materials and having meaningful discourse with other children or adults. Children need planned activities that encourage them to explore, measure, weigh, compare, and construct a variety of objects as well as ample opportunity to discuss ideas and predict solutions and reactions.

The K–4 curriculum should emphasize the development of children's mathematical thinking and reasoning abilities. For K–4, the *Standards* emphasizes the need for children to gain confidence in their abilities to think and communicate mathematically. Confident children will be better prepared to solve problems and analyze data. To develop these characteristics, the *Standards* urges "that schools build appropriate reasoning and problem-solving experiences into the curriculum (p. 18)."

The K–4 curriculum should emphasize the application of mathematics. The ultimate purpose of learning mathematical content is not to complete the exercises at the end of a textbook chapter or to pass a minimal grade competency test before June. Rather, mathematics procedures are real-world processes that help children solve problems

DEVELOPING A PLAN

in their everyday lives. Classroom activities that build on data collection and interpretation prepare children to meet these demands.

The K–4 curriculum should include a broad range of content. Careful planning is necessary to include the full spectrum of mathematical processes, especially when it is not directly laid out in mandated texts or curricula. Even young children benefit from experiences with measurement, geometry, statistics, probability, and algebra. Textbooks and curriculum guides often pay little or no attention to these branches of mathematics and teachers who are new to presenting these concepts may lack confidence in their ability to include them (or their students' capacity to comprehend them) in the primary grades. But informal introduction is not difficult.

A program based on the NCTM *Standards* will be student driven and should include a set of long-range plans that address content goals and student needs. The traditional way to use textbooks—to begin with chapter one and continue through to whatever chapter the class happens to reach at the end of the school year—does not facilitate a student-centered curriculum. This does not mean that a text is not useful. Many books, especially newer ones, have interesting activities that can be adapted to suit students' needs.

To begin the school year, teachers can develop or select instructional units that are motivating and relatively free of prerequisites. This allows the first few weeks to serve as a reentry and warm-up for students after the summer break. This also serves as an assessment period, during which the teacher can determine students' strengths and weaknesses and establish productive routines for math. After carefully watching the students in familiar situations and seeing how they work and what they are able to do, the teacher, with or without the text, is better able to map out more detailed plans related to her goals for the year, the children's needs, and local mandates.

Ms. Jackson involved her students in many patterning and graphing activities in the beginning of the year. Geometry and measurement activities also can be excellent starting points. Informal geometry is enjoyable to children and provides opportunities for patterning, comparing, analyzing, and deriving numbers from shapes.

One of Ms. Jackson's colleagues uses a highly motivating geometry activity that accomplishes two objectives. It has children investigating quantity, shape, and how objects correspond with one another, and at the same time, it establishes a routine for children to work together cooperatively. To initiate the activity, pairs of children choose seven pattern blocks of at least three different shapes. They arrange the blocks in any design or interesting shape with no interior holes. Some students create interesting symmetric and asymmetric designs; others make recognizable shapes—a vehicle, animal, or monster. After tracing around the outside of their designs, the student pairs exchange outlines and work to discover which blocks were used to create other students' designs. It isn't long before children discover that there can be more than one way to make the same design and are encouraged to discuss their findings with the original artists.

In the next step, the children try to fill in the outline with more or fewer than seven blocks. Soon numbers of edges, sizes of angles, and comparisons of shapes begin to enter into students' conversations. Finally, students devise ways to record the shapes used, the numbers of blocks, and the numbers of edges, and to compare their records with those of their classmates.

Measurement activities are a ready source of numbers for basic computation—numbers to add, subtract, compare, or use to make fractions. As Ms. Valentine observed the day her students weighed and compared their chicks (Chapter 3), when children make their own measurements and then use these measurements for problem-solving tasks, numbers, and computation take on real meaning. The activity, and therefore the numbers, are inherently motivating. Especially at the beginning of the year, measurement can be a natural extension of many "get acquainted" activities, and can be incorporated into the curriculum while familiarizing students with their new classroom environment.

Geometry, measurement, and other familiar, yet motivating, activities provide a set of lenses through which the teacher can observe the students. The teacher can ask many questions and collect and record student data. How do these children work together? What vocabulary do they incorporate into their 'math talk' and is it utilized appropriately? Are they confident in their ability to accomplish mathematical tasks? To what extent can they collect, interpret, and display data? Can they use simple problem-solving strategies? Do they have the background for the mathematical concepts we plan to cover?

Rather than placing the children within the context of a predetermined text or curriculum sequence, the teacher is then able to tailor the curriculum to the needs of the children. Starting the year with a textbook, which usually opens with one or two chapters of review,

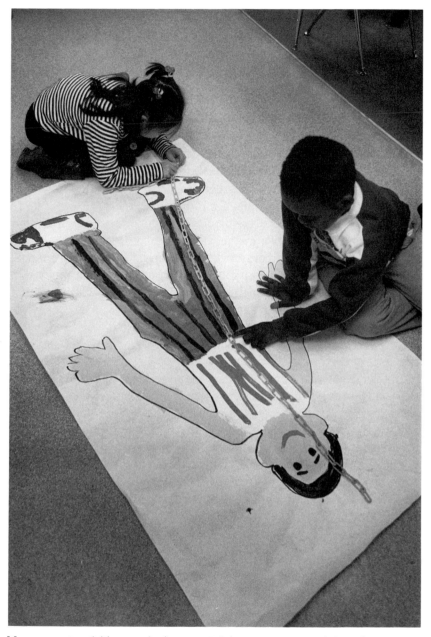

Measurement activities can be incorporated into many areas of the primary math curriculum and are a great way to integrate science, social studies, and art. They can be useful as "get acquainted" activities at the beginning of the year, and can serve as a means of assessment.

THINKING LIKE MATHEMATICIANS

does not adequately supply these important pieces of student information. In fact, opening the year with review is usually a waste of valuable instructional time. More importantly, it does not provide the motivation needed to help students move into new ideas with enthusiasm and confidence.

Once she is familiar with the skills and needs of the class, the teacher is ready to devise or adjust a long-range scheme for the year, and to project time frames for the various units she needs to cover. A long-range plan that is conceptually oriented addresses broad concepts for the students to experience over the course of the school year. Once again, the NCTM K–4 standards can assist the teacher who is new to developing this type of mathematics program.

Standards 1–4 provide a direction for instructional strategies: mathematics as problem solving; mathematics as communication; mathematics as reasoning; and mathematical connections.

Standards 5–13 list content-specific areas of mathematics education that need to be addressed in the instructional program during the K–4 years: estimation, number sense and numeration, concepts of whole number operations, whole number computation, geometry and spatial sense, measurement, statistics and probability, fractions and decimals, and patterns and relationships.

Connecting these concept areas with the text or local curriculum guidelines can help to establish a general plan for the year. A sample kindergarten plan might begin something like this:

September	October	November
geometry; games with counting; sorting, collecting & displaying data; above, below	counting activities; making sets; identifying sets by number; more, less, same; ordering sets	exploring lengths with non-standard units; comparing data

December	Ongoing	
using numerals; investigating time and money; concept of addition	language development; attendance activities; calendar activities; number sense; problem-solving skills and applications; ongoing use of previously learned concepts	

Each successive grade should go into further detail, building on content that was initiated in the previous year. A sample plan for a second-grade program might begin like this:

September	October	November
collecting and interpreting data; concept of coordinate grid; investigating numbers on a number line	using addition and subtraction in real world settings; symmetry and reflection in geometry; place value	numeration; concept of regrouping in addition and subtraction; time

December	Ongoing
measurement; addition and subtraction; interpreting bar and pictographs; concept of multiplication	calendar and attendance activities; basic fact strategies; number sense; graphing; problem solving with the development of problem strategies.

Obviously, every teacher must develop her own plan so that it can be tailored to meet the needs of her own students and curriculum. The samples provided are simply examples of what a plan might look like.

Short-Range Planning

Once the teacher has established the general conceptual framework, she can put the content into unit plans, and then select specific instructional strategies that address these major ideas.

The first step to planning a unit is to look at the math content. Specific content, often defined in the curriculum guide or textbook in terms of instructional objectives or learning outcomes, needs to be placed in the context of the students' individual needs and the specific collective needs of the class. What did students study in previous units or previous years? At what point are they functioning now? Are there linguistic or social factors that will influence learning?

The teacher can then design a plan of instructional activities that addresses concept development. This general plan need not be elaborate. It primarily serves as a guidepost that can be adjusted frequently to accommodate student progress. The teacher can often find appropriate activities in the curriculum guide, student textbook, teacher manual, or other available resources. Lessons can be adapted to fit the needs of each class population.

Teachers who primarily use textbooks as entry points for their scope and sequence plans can still creatively adapt text activities to their individual classroom needs. Consider, for example, a textbook that describes an outdoor activity in which children make a variety of triangles and quadrilaterals and then record their characteristics. Children, representing vertices (corners), hold a rope, linking themselves together. They record in pictures the many kinds of triangles and quadrilaterals they can make with a given length of rope.

Even though the curriculum guide and text recommend beginning the year with recognition of numerals, a teacher in northern Minnesota might need to use this geometry activity in September, before the weather gets too cold for children to be outdoors. She might choose to do the activity in the fall and use the recorded pictures for a classroom introduction to the meaning and symbolic representation of 3 and 4. The recorded shapes can be duplicated with three and four rods of various lengths in the classroom. After other numerals have been introduced, the children can continue the outdoor activity by making models of polygons with 5, 6, 7, or more sides and vertices. The teacher can use the recorded results to help young children investigate order (more than, less than, the same as), addition and subtraction facts, and even measurement and identification of various polygons in the world about them.

To add challenge to the activity, the teacher might encourage the children to use combinations of two or more pattern blocks to make a variety of shapes with four, five, six, or more sides. Or they could use the rope to investigate shapes with no corners. How would they hold the rope to make these shapes? How many such shapes can there be? Could they create a shape with one or two corners?

In "interpreting" unit plans into daily activities, careful attention must be given to how well a selected activity brings out the mathematics. In classrooms incorporating the *Standards,* teachers usually provide several hands-on experiences with concrete materials before pencil-and-paper activity, and allow ample opportunity for students to discuss individual problem-solving strategies with other children and interested adults.

Although it's true that children have the greatest opportunity to build accurate and useful mathematics concepts when the activities are engaging and developmentally appropriate, many "fun" activities have little mathematical potential. In other activities, the mathematical potential may not be realized unless the teacher carefully thinks it through in advance, and uses good questions to promote thoughtful discussion. For instance, students enjoy using base-ten blocks to perform addition or subtraction, but they may need direction in making the connection between the block activity and the algorithm as it is recorded on paper.

If this connection is not made, the blocks become a separate algorithm; they become a burden rather than a support.

Many teachers find it beneficial to begin each unit with a day of activities that review concepts essential to understanding the unit. This can serve two purposes: students can remember and sharpen previously acquired content knowledge by revisiting old concepts, and the teacher can assess the students' present functional level. Test results and anecdotal records that show student achievement at the end of a previous instructional unit may no longer hold true, since children often grow in conceptual understanding without the aid of direct instruction.

As Ms. Jackson discovered, planning daily lessons should not be done too far in advance because plans need to be regularly revised. Armed with information gained through informal daily assessment, she fine-tunes her plans every one or two days. Should this activity be extended? For whom was it too difficult? Who needs additional support? Are the students bored and ready to move on to more challenging problems?

Sticking to the Plan

Each teacher needs to experiment with different methods of mathematics planning in order to find the best course of action for her teaching approach and classroom situation. Teachers new to the methods set forth in the NCTM *Standards* may find that failure to establish a strong long-range plan can increase the risk they will drop their newfound approach.

Traditional direct instruction often brings tangible, testable (albeit sometimes fleeting) results early in the school year, and teachers used to more didactic teaching methods initially may be alarmed by a lack of concrete evidence of student achievement. Midway through the first year of her new program, Ms. Jackson began to worry. She remembered student test and drill performances of previous years. This year's students appeared less proficient in pencil-and-paper computation. It was clear she was not moving through the curriculum as rapidly as before, and she worried that her class would not make it through the year's math program.

But then she remembered that in other years she had given her students facts to memorize, clearly defined algorithms to use, and specific skills to perform. They retained less, and were not able to discuss what they were doing. Now, while providing them with a strong mathematics foundation, progress was taking a little more time and was a little more difficult to ascertain.

As her January money unit rolled around, she noticed how smoothly it went. Students were better prepared to tackle the most difficult aspects of the unit than students in previous years. Other math content areas seemed to benefit equally. She noticed that students used the vocabulary of math throughout the day and that they appeared self-assured and confident in their abilities to solve problems.

A different kind of progress was taking hold. After careful observation and student-teacher discussions, Ms. Jackson realized that her students had a deeper conceptual understanding and were better able to transfer that understanding to new situations.

Before long, students were producing positive, testable results, and she was surprised to discover that her class covered all the mandated content objectives with time to spare. Given the opportunity to build concepts, habits, and confidence early, her students were able to move quickly through the more difficult units they encountered later in the year. This was an added bonus for her—one that she cashed in on by letting her students explore unscheduled content areas, solve logic problems, and play math games.

Giving students the opportunity to develop concepts and their own methods of solving problems requires patience, flexibility, and time. The payoff is better mathematical concept development. Once students have established basic math concepts, they will move through the curriculum more quickly, with greater confidence, and with a higher rate of success.

Spontaneity vs. Planning

A student-centered curriculum that gives learners the opportunity to develop their own methods of solving problems in meaningful situations necessitates flexible planning. Often the greatest motivation to learn occurs as a result of spontaneous events that happen in and around the classroom. At the same time, mathematics instruction cannot be totally extemporaneous and unplanned.

Occasionally, teachers modify their daily plans to take advantage of unexpected events, but they might want to think about why they developed a plan in the first place. Long-range planning is essential to implementing a program that encourages students to think mathematically. Educators agree that mathematics has a specific body of content that should be developed in a planned sequence, and teachers who use

Like those in Ms. Jackson's class, students who are given the opportunity to build a strong mathematics foundation are able to tackle difficult problems with confidence.

a long-range plan for the year can safely assume that an adequate range of important ideas is being explored.

When planning relies too heavily on serendipity and too little on adherence to a logical mathematical sequence, mathematics learning can get off track. It becomes easy to miss or gloss over content in an attempt to seize the opportunity of the moment. However, if the long-range plan is firmly established, and the desired learning outcomes continue to guide activities, it becomes easy to adapt daily lessons to fit timely topics. Place value, fractions, or statistics can be taught in the context of current events—the Olympic games, a new class pet, or even a news event that has affected families in the community.

Planning for Math in an Integrated Curriculum

Placing mathematics instruction within the context of other curricular areas helps make sense of math concepts, establishes a value for math content, and gives meaning to the other disciplines. Thematic planning—planning interdisciplinary units around broad or specific themes (transportation, raising baby chicks, setting up a recycling project) can incorporate math, science, reading, language arts, and social studies, as well as art, music, and physical education. Math can serve as a tool to make sense of the other areas. Students use measurement, graphing, and statistics to collect, record, and interpret social and scientific data. The use of fractions, estimation, and number operations are inherent in scientific procedures.

The scope and sequence of the math content should be evident in the overall plan in an integrated curriculum. Often it is the science or social studies that drives an interdisciplinary unit and math becomes a peripheral issue. If, for example, a teacher chooses a weather topic as the theme for a unit, he may concentrate on the science content and use reading, writing, and math as tools to accomplish specific science objectives. Math may be used every day during this unit, but unless the specific mathematics concepts defined in the long-range plan are addressed, the students may fail to progress mathematically.

But frequently, the sequence of the science content is less critical than the sequence of the mathematics content. Specific objectives in a weather unit, for example, can be studied at any point in the year. To most effectively develop the potential of the mathematics involved in this unit, formal weather study might be shifted to the latter half of the year, when students have had many experiences with fractions, graphing, and measurement, and are ready for a unit on interrelating units of measurement. Of course, as with many areas of mathematics, some of the weather objectives might best be spread over the school year, and tied into other curricular areas accordingly. By looking carefully at the skills needed in a science or social studies unit, and then matching them with the skills the students have acquired and/or are currently working on, teachers can develop interdisciplinary units that enhance both the mathematics curriculum and the other content areas.

7

IMPLEMENTING THE PROGRAM

Rosa, Tyrone, and the other children described in this text attend schools that are implementing the NCTM *Standards* in their math curriculum. These schools are located in a fairly typical urban area, where teachers and children must cope daily with the socioeconomic effects associated with low-income districts. But despite the environment around these schools, students are achieving in math. Teachers are rethinking their strategies, restocking their shelves and cupboards, and retooling their classrooms to address the goals set by the *Standards*. Most of all, these teachers are proving that these methods can be implemented in any school or classroom.

If the best elements from each of these schools were combined, they would form a model school-community committed to excellence in mathematics—a school in which children are encouraged to value and use math in personal terms.

What might a visitor walking down the hall of a model school find? Brightly decorated walls sporting student art and colorful posters, many displaying mathematics concepts. Outside one first-grade class, the hum of children's voices is punctuated by an occasional exclamation or laugh. The teacher's voice can be heard in gentle conversation with several children, rising in inquiry and then pausing as the smaller voices respond.

A peek inside reveals walls covered with charts, graphs, posters, and calendars. Magnetic name tags are distributed across three sectors of an attendance Venn diagram. Clear containers holding various blocks, links, and cubes are stacked on shelves beside books, microscopes, geoboards, and several sets of scales. The children, huddled in small groups, bend intently over their work.

A closer examination reveals the source of their activity. Each group shares a colorfully sewn cloth sack, bulging with blocks. One partner shakes the bag and the second reaches in and pulls out a block. Another child records its color on a graph and returns the block to the bag. The teacher visits each group and asks questions that help the students see relationships among collected data. "What color block did you get the most of?" "Why do you think that happened?" "Which color did you get the least of?" "Do you think there are more red, blue, or yellow blocks in the bag?" "Why?" "If you did this again, which color do you think you'd pull out most often?" "Now fill a bag and predict what color blocks you would choose most often."

Continuing on through the school wing, a visitor might note the variety of lessons and learning strategies evident in the classrooms. In one room children are busy writing and exchanging their own addition story problems, while the class next door works on place value. These children are working with base-ten blocks using numbers that came from a physical education activity. In another classroom, children are voting on the book they'll be reading later that day and using Post-it™ notes to add their names to a wall chart. In still another class, busy hands deftly measure desks, books, and cubbies, and then record the data in notebooks.

Naturally, each activity has been set up differently. Student background experiences, performance levels, and personalities vary. Teachers put their own signatures on their programs in ways that highlight individual preferences and strengths. But, despite the obvious differences, there are key elements common to all classrooms successfully implementing the NCTM *Standards*. In these classrooms, teachers informally assess student progress throughout the day. They take care to value each child's learning style and individual approach to math problems, no matter how far from the traditional path it may wind. In addition, these mathematics programs have children

- solving problems in meaningful situations
- using manipulatives
- working cooperatively with others in small groups
- developing their own procedures, which they can discuss, explain, modify, write about, and value
- using thinking strategies to learn basic facts
- encountering math throughout their curriculum—in language and reading, social studies and science, and even art and physical education.

Evidence of mathematics can be found everywhere in schools implementing the NCTM Standards.

SOLVING PROBLEMS IN MEANINGFUL SITUATIONS

Solving problems must be the focus of any mathematics instruction program. Teachers will see in the NCTM *Standards* that problem solving is "standard number one," which states that

> in grades K–4, the study of mathematics should emphasize problem solving so that students can
>
> - use problem-solving approaches to investigate and understand mathematical content;
> - formulate problems from everyday and mathematical situations;
> - develop and apply strategies to solve a wide variety of problems;
> - verify and interpret results with respect to the original problem;
> - acquire confidence in using mathematics meaningfully.
>
> (p. 23)

Children need to be placed in problem-solving situations that lead them to develop their own ideas and understandings. In the early grades, these can come directly from the students' daily routines and experiences. Such child-centered situations appeal to the inherent ego-centricity of youngsters, and they encourage students to see the value of mathematics in their everyday lives.

It is the teacher's role to select or create activities that will be meaningful for her students and then flush out the mathematical possibilities from these activities. Real-world activities such as cooking; building something for the classroom; or selecting, dividing, and distributing materials for a class party are examples that are inherently of interest to children and hold tremendous instructional possibilities (see Figure 7–1).

Being receptive to student-generated questions can lead teachers to the most meaningful activities of all. As children investigate their own questions at their own pace, they are primed for discovery; they seek meaning in their own worlds. Time spent thoroughly investigating a few high-interest problems can prove to be more productive than completing many low-interest problems that do not incorporate adequate discussion about discoveries, processes, and results.

"Meaningful problems" do not always need to be real world problems, but instead could be those that utilize manipulative materials, such as pattern blocks or tangrams; story problems; or activities that connect math with other disciplines. When the students in one class graphed the vowels and consonants in their spelling lists, they became curious whether there was a pattern from one week's list to the next. The

IMPLEMENTING THE PROGRAM

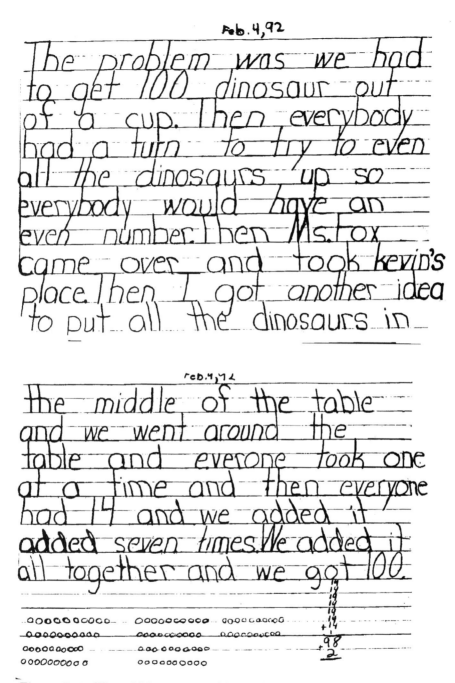

Feb. 4, 92

The problem was we had to get 100 dinosaur out of a cup. Then everybody had a turn to try to even all the dinosaurs up so everybody would have an even number. Then Ms. Fox came over and took kevin's place. Then I got another idea to put all the dinosaurs in

Feb. 4, 92

the middle of the table and we went around the table and everone took one at a time and then everyone had 14 and we added it added seven times. We added it all together and we got 100.

Figure 7–1 *When children are placed in creative problem-solving situations, they are driven to develop their own procedures, ideas, and understandings.*

ensuing investigation was taken on by a small group of children who shared their findings with the rest of the class, updating their data weekly.

Story problems are often used to motivate specific areas of mathematics content and require the development of specific problem-solving strategies. For example, one difficult subtraction situation for primary-grade children occurs when the starting number is unknown. Students might be given a problem like, "Alice had some toy dinosaurs. She gave eight to Jeremy. Now Alice has fifteen dinosaurs. How many did she have to start with?" Helping children learn that they could draw a picture to depict the events of the story not only helps them solve the problem, but it helps them value problem-solving strategies. This question could be treated initially as an art activity and could incorporate various number combinations.

No matter how motivating or interesting the setting, one should not assume that children will automatically get mathematical meaning from every classroom activity. Frequent teacher-student, student-student, and whole-group discussions assist both conceptual understanding and language development, often with the teacher guiding the direction of the discussions through thoughtful comments and probing questions. Students become independent thinkers and problem solvers when they are prodded with open-ended questions: "What strategies do you think might work to find a solution?" "What were you thinking when you solved that problem?" "Is your answer reasonable and how can you decide if it is?"

USING MANIPULATIVES

Learning theory suggests that children's mathematics knowledge originates with their actions upon objects. Conceptual understanding moves from the concrete (working with objects) to the semiconcrete (pictorial or representational) to the abstract (mental or symbolic).

Many children learn to identify numerals, or can rote count to relatively high numbers at an early age. "Five," exclaims one young child when shown that numeral. "Hear me count," commands another who proceeds in rapid fire, "one, two, three, four, five." Despite these early performances, many teachers (and even many parents) realize that young children have little "number sense," that they don't fully understand numbers and number processes. Before children can *understand* 5, they must first discover "fiveness." They must encounter multiple sets of five—five blocks, five crayons, five shoes, five children. They must handle five, they must count five, they must be able to divide it up, and then put it back together again. They must associate in one-to-one correspondence five cookies, five plates, and five children. In essence, they cannot understand the abstract meaning of five, or even associate what the numeral 5 represents, until they have had multiple experiences with concrete objects and many opportunities to relate 5 to other numbers.

Manipulatives provide the props with which children explore mathematics concepts. With concrete materials in hand, they can experiment, build, add, divide, weigh, measure, and compare. They can develop and apply abstract ideas, make hypotheses, and test ideas. They have props that invite reflection, stimulate and facilitate conversation, and assist explanation.

A variety of materials should be available for children as they move through their mathematics program. The NCTM *Standards* suggests that primary-grade classrooms be equipped with counters; interlocking cubes; connecting links; base-ten, attribute, and pattern blocks; tiles; geometric models; rulers; spinners; colored rods; geoboards; balances; fraction pieces; and graph, grid, and dot paper.

While more expensive materials are often kept in a central location so that classrooms can share their use, a variety of items needs to be kept in each classroom so children can benefit from daily use. For example, connecting cubes in kindergarten and first grade, or place value materials in first through third grades, should be available for easy access.

For the many schools that do not have the funds to equip each room with all supplies, homemade materials can prove to be as good as or better than those produced commercially. For example, dried lima beans spray painted on one side make excellent two-color counters. Having children or their families contribute or even construct materials is a fun and easy way to get parents, grandparents, and even siblings involved. Constructing materials, which often involves measurement and computation skills, offers the added benefit of providing valuable learning experiences for children at home or in school.

Students who have little or no experience using manipulatives will probably require some special support before they use the materials effectively. Many children, for example, misunderstand base-ten blocks. Some of these students see ten ones glued together as just another "single" block of a different size. These children are simply not ready

Manipulative materials provide the props with which children can experiment, build, add, divide, weigh, measure, and compare.

to use the blocks. Others have not had enough experience with the blocks to understand the place value arrangement from ones to tens to hundreds. They will need more help from teachers and other students to interpret the blocks before they can use them effectively.

Using manipulatives often requires, and can be used to help develop, student responsibility. Some materials, such as the rubber bands used with geoboards, seem to lend themselves to misuse. Many teachers have found that pairing students who are more easily distracted with those who are more responsible may ward off problems before they begin and enforcing a strict "misuse leads to no use" policy usually alleviates problems (with time). In any event, as students become more familiar with the daily use of geoboards, blocks, and links, the novelty of handling materials diminishes and more time and energy can be devoted to their application in a creative and interesting mathematics learning environment.

Introducing manipulatives one at a time gives children a chance to become familiar with the characteristics and uses of each new set of materials. Students need time to explore the manipulatives on their own before being asked to use the materials in activities designated by the teacher. Some teachers ask students to think of as many uses as they can for new materials. This enhances student exploration, and allows children a chance to gain confidence without experiencing stress or failure. Additionally, observing students while they explore can provide the teacher with insight into the children's mathematical maturity and individual creativity. (This is also an appropriate time for teachers to establish ground rules or for students to get some of the less mathematical "experimenting" out of the way.)

Having students take turns distributing, checking, and collecting materials on a daily basis helps build responsibility. Wall charts and daily assignment cards can be used to assign and keep track of whose job it is to pass out or clean up materials. Proper storage helps ease the distribution and collection of materials. Lunch trays or sample carpet squares prevent pieces from falling off desks and can reduce the noise associated with students working with blocks on a hard surface.

Assigning children to pairs or small groups often facilitates classroom management. It allows the teacher to work with fewer children at a time, helps her monitor the use of materials, and makes it easier to monitor student understanding. In classrooms that are not well equipped, this method also reduces the quantity of materials needed for the group.

It must be noted that providing manipulative materials is not educational in and of itself. Children must be placed in meaningful situations—those that pose interesting problems and provide opportunities for personal reflection and peer interaction—for concrete materials to foster growth in mathematics concepts.

WORKING COOPERATIVELY

Math is not a spectator sport. In order to learn mathematics, children need to be active participants in doing and discussing mathematics. Working in pairs and/or small groups, then, is almost essential to the most effective student learning. Because children are naturally social, group processes can easily play a fundamental part in primary grade mathematics programs. They enable each child to speak, listen, and work cooperatively with others in the learning process.

Traditional classrooms have one speaker (often the teacher or a highly verbal child) and twenty-five or so listeners. In these scenarios, only one child is an active participant, while all others are relegated to the passive role of listeners (if they are even doing that). Child-centered classrooms often function under a different model, incorporating cooperative grouping activities throughout the day. When a class of twenty-four students is divided into groups of two or four, there can be up to twelve speakers actively involved at any one time, and twelve listeners poised and ready to respond.

Cooperative learning strategies provide opportunities to grow socially, analytically, and conceptually. Solving problems with others demands that students inquire, explore, analyze, explain, challenge, justify, modify, interpret and communicate their ideas effectively, working together to solve a common problem.

Group activities can lead to a better development of mathematical understanding because of the communication that must occur for the group to function. Ideally, these activities necessitate that children use all four components of language skills: speaking, listening, reading, and writing. As children communicate in a mathematical problem-solving activity, they must incorporate the language of math. They break down intuitive thoughts into step-by-step plans and processes, concretizing concepts for themselves as they explain them to others. Planning action, making diagrams, describing shapes, comparing sizes, predicting outcomes, and explaining solutions requires students to make the kind of connections between abstract concepts and verbal or graphic symbols that build a strong mathematical foundation.

Children's independence and interdependence in learning mathematics are nurtured by group work. Collaborating with peers gives students a chance to work out mathematical problems cooperatively. They are able to reason in nonthreatening situations, explore ideas together, experiment with various strategies, and concur on conclusions. Group members must explain and defend their partially formed ideas, while interpreting those of their peers and accepting alternative solutions. Best of all, they learn that they can help one another to succeed without having to rely on an external "expert."

Implementing student grouping requires active teacher participation. As children work in their groups, the teacher can move around the classroom to monitor progress by observing, listening, and asking questions. In so doing, he will become aware of which children most need his attention. He will know whether their needs primarily involve math content, language development, self-confidence, or group skills, and can tailor his directions, questioning, and interaction to best suit each child.

When children have not worked in groups previously, it might be best to start with pairs, rather than groups of three or four. Primary-grade children often work better with one partner than in larger groups, and in the beginning at least, cooperative habits might best be established in the smallest possible group combinations. When larger groups are necessary, some teachers assign roles—note taker, discussion leader, materials monitor, reporter. The teacher can foster independence by letting children know what is expected of them, thus enabling them to perform the appropriate tasks involved in their role. When tasks are rotated daily or weekly, each child has a chance to contribute in a variety of ways.

Collaborative activity demands that *all* members participate and progress, so although children have individual tasks to perform, they develop a sense of group responsibility. Groups must work together, making sure that each member understands the mathematics process involved. Rotating the role of group "presenter" requires that each member understand the process and actively participate, at least some of the time.

As with manipulatives, effective group work does not happen magically. It requires persistence and patience by teachers and students alike. Many teachers who successfully implement cooperative groups in their classrooms often incorporate a common set of elements into their programs. They make sure that they establish interesting and worthwhile tasks, activities, and problems for the groups to work on; they have a clearly defined set of classroom procedures that they stick to consistently and fairly; and they become active participants themselves, moving freely among the groups, entering into discussions, adding probing questions, and subtly facilitating the group process. (This also provides an opportunity to informally assess student understanding.)

Needless to say, as students become involved in tasks that they find interesting and understandable, the "busy noise" of activity is everywhere. Teachers, administrators, and classroom visitors need to be prepared for the sounds of *constructive noise* and understand that when children are working and talking in groups, the noise level will be higher than in a classroom in which children are more passive. Many teachers find it helpful to develop strategies that gain the attention of the whole group, perhaps by using hand signals or flicking the lights. Once students are accustomed to these strategies, they usually become quiet within a few seconds of the teacher's signal.

VALUING STUDENT-DEVELOPED PROCEDURES

"How did you do that—what was your thinking?" is a question often repeated in these classrooms. Teachers need to encourage students to develop their own procedures, and then provide supportive opportunities for children to verbalize their approaches.

Children learn best when they actively build their own mathematical procedures and understandings, not when they simply sit back and receive information from teacher or text. Reliance on teacher-prescribed algorithms does little to foster procedural understanding. When constructing their own knowledge, children develop strategies that they understand, believe in, can duplicate, and can explain through speaking and writing.

Many skills and understandings, particularly those associated with primary grades, can be developed by the students themselves if they are asked to solve meaningful problems. Developed in this way, these mathematics skills provide a strong foundation and lend a sense of ownership for the students.

Teachers can regularly ask children to explain their thinking. This is worthwhile for both "right" and "wrong" responses, as long as the teacher takes care not to make correctness seem the point of the exercise. Frequently, children will see where they went astray as they

The availability of a variety of math materials helps ensure opportunities for children to develop their own procedures with understanding.

explain a "wrong" answer and will correct themselves in the process of their explanation.

When children explain their thinking to others, they personalize and concretize their own knowledge. Verbalizing one's thinking requires organization and understanding. It creates ownership of concepts. Often, children arrive at a correct answer intuitively, and are unaware of the specific mathematical procedures they applied. When they explain a solution, they are required to break that intuitive process into discrete steps and justify it. Their explanation, therefore, pushes them to develop a plan that they can use and modify each time they encounter a similar problem. In essence, they build their own algorithm. Sometimes, however, the explanation does not provide a replicable process by which to find a correct answer.

Kevin was given a story problem to solve about a girl at the fair. The problem was quite complicated for a second grader, and involved two rides, the number of tickets required for each ride, and the amount of time each ride lasted. Kevin needed to determine how many tickets the girl in the story would need if she wanted to ride each ride for six minutes. It took him very little time to solve the problem and give a correct answer.

"How did you do that, Kevin?" asked his teacher. "What was your thinking?"

Kevin launched into an explanation, but his method was faulty and was obviously leading him to a wrong answer. About halfway through his explanation, he stopped, realizing he was on the wrong track. He was stuck.

The teacher remained silent. She did not make a suggestion. She did not call on another child to help get Kevin back on track. She did not even ask if he needed help. She simply waited and allowed him the time to think.

After about thirty seconds, Kevin exclaimed, "Oh, now I know!" He started over and explained a logical procedure that produced the correct answer.

As children explain their thinking—describe how they got a handle on a problem and solved it on their own—they are confirmed as mathematicians. They gain self-confidence. They are empowered to make their own decisions, find solutions, determine for themselves if they are right or wrong. As happened with Kevin, explaining an answer often helps children clarify a fuzzy idea about the method they used to reach a solution. Assured that their teacher values each idea, student mathematicians feel free to think creatively, and can then express their procedures openly. In turn, they learn to value the ideas of their classmates.

Upon completion of a lesson in which children have solved problems individually or in small groups, it is often productive to meet again in a whole-class format, allowing students the opportunity to share their procedures and ideas with the rest of the group. This not only provides closure for the lesson, it lets children listen to the wide variety of ways that any one problem can be solved. Students hear strategies that they may not have thought of on their own and, as they listen to their classmates, they must interpret and modify these other explanations in terms of their own constructs of understanding.

During these whole-class discussions, it is essential for *all* students to participate regularly. By repeatedly calling on only those who raise their hands, a teacher excludes the very students who most need to build confidence in their math, language, and social skills. In group discussions, usually the easiest concepts are contributed first. As an alternative to calling on hand-wavers, many teachers choose to connect first with those students weakest in their mathematics understanding or those who have difficulty communicating their ideas. Participating *first* allows these children to successfully contribute to group discussions, thus nurturing language and confidence in those students who may need this type of support. Additionally, this approach leaves the more complex concepts for the highly verbal and/or mathematically advanced students, and encourages them to stretch their own understanding and communication skills.

USING THINKING STRATEGIES TO LEARN BASIC FACTS

Do you know the state capital of Wyoming, or the state bird? What is New Mexico's primary agricultural crop? These are not easy questions if you've forgotten your old geography facts. What can you do if you don't have the resources to look up the answers? Not much!

Now, what if you don't remember the sum of 3 + 4? How could you figure out the answer? Well, you could count on your fingers; or combine a group of three pencils with a group of four to represent the problem; or think of a fact that you do remember, such as 3 + 3, and add 1 to it. You might remember that 4 + 3 = 7, and realize that 3 + 4 must equal the same number. In other words, when a child knows the many strategies that can be applied to determine a math fact, it is not difficult for her to derive the answer.

When children rote memorize facts, they have nothing to fall back on when they later forget those facts. In the same way that committing fifty state capitals to memory contributes little to an understanding of government, the memorization of addition tables provides no understanding of math processes, no familiarity with addition concepts, and no safety net when memory fails. But children can develop basic strategies to help them discover answers for addition, subtraction, and even multiplication and division problems. Best of all, as they use these strategies in frequent and appropriate problem-solving situations, children eventually remember the facts naturally, without stress or fear of failure. Research indicates that meaningful learning of facts is much more efficient than rote recall (Thornton and Smith 1988; Fuson 1986).

Perhaps the most basic and the most powerful strategies for deriving addition or subtraction facts are "counting on" and "counting back." For example, when adding 8 + 3, the child starts at 8, and "counts on" three more—9, 10, 11. Although this strategy seems obvious, to many children it is not. Learning that they should start with the larger number, whether it is on the right or the left, enables them to use this procedure easily. The problem 3 + 8 is the same as 8 + 3. When children understand counting on, and know they can reverse number order, they can figure out any simple addition problem they encounter.

There are also certain fact patterns that children find easy to learn. "Doubles," such as 5 + 5 or 6 + 6, seem more easily learned than other number combinations. Using the more easily remembered facts and then coupling them with other strategies, such as counting on, allows children to figure out other combinations. A child who cannot remember the answer to 5 + 6, for example, may remember 5 + 5 = 10, and then can count on one more to get 11.

There is no doubt that learning basic facts is essential to gaining math power. It is important that students know their facts and can apply them to problem-solving, mental arithmetic and estimation situations. But memorizing facts without a means of deriving a forgotten fact robs students of control, and the very power that lets them view themselves as mathematicians.

To develop this necessary knowledge, students must continually be placed in situations in which they both need to know and have the means to determine, simple facts. Over time, they will commit the facts to memory—naturally. Teachers can use a variety of methods to help children learn basic addition facts. Games that require adding the dots

Children can be challenged to learn math facts in fun and meaningful ways.

on a set of dice before moving a game piece are fun and motivating. Such games should be based on random chance so that all students, not just the most capable, have an equal opportunity to win. Working with manipulatives often requires combining numbers to find totals. Combining sets of unifix cubes and adding and recording the numbers of sides on geometric pattern blocks are but two exercises that provide hands-on activity and plenty of repetition and practice. Classroom problems, such as those requiring students to determine the number of cookies needed for two tables of children, are real-world situations in which the combination of numbers has real purpose, and consequently, real meaning.

Ms. Valentine has found that fun fact activities can be connected with other curricular areas, especially art. One activity enables her to draw connections among math doubles, fractions, and symmetry (see Figure 7–2). Building on ideas from *Moving into Math* (Irons and Trafton 1992), she has the children fold paper to show two halves. (The halves can be as simple as torn squares, or as fancy as cut paper butterflies.) On one

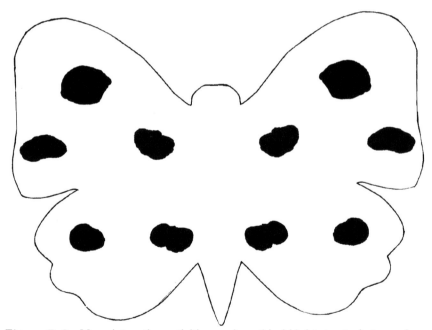

Figure 7–2 *Many interesting activities, such as this folded paper project, can be adapted to help children with math concepts.*

half, the children place a given number of dots of tempera paint. Then, quickly, before the paint can dry, they fold the dry half over onto the painted half.

"Can you predict how many dots will show when the paper is unfolded?" Ms. Valentine asks the children. Having answered, they unfold, counting if necessary, and see if they were correct.

Students keep their papers for reference and review of addition doubles. Sometimes, they add more dots in different colors (especially effective with folded butterflies) so they can then refer to the numbers of "pink dots," "yellow dots," or the total number of dots on the paper.

Ms. Valentine has even developed a means to use the painted dots for subtraction. She has the children count the total number of dots on the unfolded paper. Then they predict how many will be on one side. To check their prediction, they fold the paper and count the dots on one half.

Timed drills or drill and practice worksheets do not assist "math with meaning" learning. They merely contribute to math anxiety and a decline of interest in math learning. Children can be challenged to learn their math facts in fun and meaningful ways. These will enable them to develop strategies that will stay with them as they move into more complex and demanding mathematical procedures. Some of the fact strategies appropriate for grades K–4 include the following:

ADDITION AND SUBTRACTION

Counting on	1, 2, 3
Turning a fact around	$3 + 8 = 8 + 3$ (addition only)
Doubles	$8 + 8 = 16$
	$16 - 8 = 8$
Doubles + 1	$7 + 8 = 7 + 7 + 1$
Sum of 10	$6 + 4 = 10$
Sum of 10 + 1	$6 + 5 = 6 + 4 + 1$
Compensation	$8 + 6 = (8 - 1) + (6 + 1) = 7 + 7$

MULTIPLICATION

Relate to repeated addition	$4 \times 3 = 3 + 3 + 3 + 3$
Visualize as an array	□ □ □ □ □ □
	□ □ □ □ □ □

Facts of 2 and 5 by skip counting	$2, 4, 6, 8, 10 \ldots$ $5, 10, 15, 20 \ldots$
Building facts of 3 on those of 2	$3 \times 4 = (2 \times 4) + 4$
Building facts of 4 by doubling those of 2	$4 \times 6 = (2 \times 6) \times 2$
Building facts of 6 on those of 5	$6 \times 3 = (5 \times 3) + 3$
Building facts of 6 by doubling those of 3	$6 \times 7 = (3 \times 7) \times 2$
Building facts of 4 on those of 5	$4 \times 7 = (5 \times 7) - 7$
Turning a fact around	$7 \times 4 = 4 \times 7$
Seeing a pattern in the facts for 9 (there are many)	Sum of the digits in the products always equals 9. Tens digits increase by 1 as the ones digits decrease by 1. (45, 54, 63, 72)

ENCOUNTERING MATH THROUGHOUT THE CURRICULUM

It almost goes without saying that in order to encourage children to value mathematics, they must see that it is useful throughout the curriculum, throughout the day. Math talk should be standard for students' complete language development, not just for a one-hour math class each morning. Math principles must provide the foundation for collecting, recording, and interpreting information from the other content areas.

Daily routines are rife with math potential. Many teachers like to use attendance each morning to reinforce mathematics. Students can place magnetic name tags or Post-it™ notes on a graph or a Venn diagram when they enter the room in the morning. Those not placing their marker (after a reminder, if necessary) are the students who are absent. A Venn diagram for attendance could use the statements, "I took a bus to school," "I rode in a car," "I walked to school," to require children to make complex decisions about where to place their marker if, for example, their dad gave them a ride to the bus stop.

Teachers who look for opportunities to use math throughout the day find that there is no subject that cannot be incorporated into, or benefit from, mathematics: weighing, measuring, recording, and interpreting

Using a Venn diagram for attendance creates opportunities for class discussion.

science data; graphing statistics gathered in social studies; predicting or comparing story information to bridge from reading to writing; preparing and distributing art materials, or measuring distances or recording statistics in physical education activities. Every curricular area benefits from mathematical exploration.

THINKING LIKE MATHEMATICIANS

8

EVALUATION

*D*r. Will Smith, the local math supervisor, was observing Ms. Lorraine Howard's second-grade class. When he arrived, the children were just completing a "favorite flavor graph," which charted several flavors of ice cream and each child's favorite. Anxious to highlight the good thinking that was going on in her class, Ms. Howard said to the children, "Look at the graph and tell me something you see up there." Immediately several hands went up in the air.

"Most kids like chocolate the best," said one girl.

"Who can tell me something different?" the teacher asked.

"Nobody likes banana flavor," said a boy.

"Toni and I were the only ones who liked orange sherbet. More people liked vanilla," another child observed.

"Great. Can anyone tell me something different?" persisted Ms. Howard, trying to ferret out every idea.

"I see a pattern the way people like the flavors," ventured another boy.

"Tell us your pattern, Jeffrey," responded Ms. Howard.

Jeffrey proceeded to give a literal description of the graph: "Two kids like orange sherbet, lots liked chocolate, but Charise was the only one who liked bubble gum. Me, Anthony, Jon, and Adelle like cookie dough. That's four. And nobody liked banana and three liked vanilla." His answer appeared to tell nothing about patterns. Ms. Howard seemed embarrassed that this student demonstrated such a lack of understanding in front of the math supervisor, but Dr. Smith's enthusiasm was undampened.

"This is great!" he exclaimed. "Look at what you've just learned about the children and that child in particular! He obviously knows that there is something called a 'pattern,' and he wants to learn about it, but he needs help in doing that. If you've provided the students with activities that had them patterning earlier this year, it's clear that he didn't yet grasp the concept."

"At some point in the future," Dr. Smith continued, "you may want to see if Jeffrey can extend a pattern that someone else has started. That would be a prerequisite to creating a pattern of his own. You might also want to see if he and the others in the class can find patterns that are embedded in larger groupings that don't have a pattern. Of course, children may see real patterns where we don't, so it's vital to let them explain their thinking in this activity."

This story underscores a central theme in new approaches to assessment. Assessment can take place at any time, in any situation; it is often more accurate when noted in nontest situations; and, most importantly, it is an essential tool for guiding the direction of instruction. Evaluation can be a formative process, one that determines where children's strengths and weaknesses are. As such, it guides instruction, and, at the end of instruction, indicates the strengths and weaknesses of the instructional process itself.

Assessment goes hand in hand with instruction, so when instructional practices change, the forms of assessment and evaluation must change also. To this end, the NCTM *Standards* places strong emphasis on evaluative practices. So strong, in fact, that it devotes an entire section, and fourteen individual items, to evaluation standards. The evaluation standards reflect the need to break with tradition and focus on assessing outcomes in which students become mathematicians—actually "do" mathematics. Specific shifts of emphasis in evaluation practices are clearly defined in the table (see p. 93) printed in the *Standards:*

The *Standards* states:

> In an instructional environment that demands a deeper understanding of mathematics, testing instruments that call for only the identification of single correct responses no longer suffice. Instead, our instruments must reflect the scope and intent of our instructional program to have students solve problems, reason, and communicate. Furthermore, the instruments must enable the teacher to understand students' perceptions of mathematical ideas and processes and their ability to function in a mathematical context. At the same time, they must be sensitive enough to help teachers identify individual areas of difficulty in order to improve instruction (p. 192).

The diversity of instructional practices recommended by the NCTM *Standards* is reflected by an equal diversity in recommended forms of assessment. Assessments can be formal or informal and can take place in almost any setting. They can be implemented individually or in small or large groups. Evaluation can be presented in many ways: oral, written, demonstration, or even computer-based formats. Appropriate

Increased Attention	Decreased Attention
• Assessing what students know and how they think about mathematics	• Assessing what students do not know
• Having assessment be an integral part of teaching	• Having assessment be simply counting correct answers on tests for the sole purpose of assigning grades
• Focusing on a broad range of mathematical tasks and taking a holistic view of mathematics	• Focusing on a large number of specific and isolated skills organized by a content-behavior matrix
• Developing problem situations that require the applications of a number of mathematical ideas	• Using exercises or word problems requiring only one or two skills
• Using multiple assessment techniques, including written, oral, and demonstration formats	• Using only written tests
• Using calculators, computers, and manipulatives in assessment	• Excluding calculators, computers, and manipulatives from the assessment process
• Evaluating the program by systematically collecting information on outcomes, curriculum, and instruction	• Evaluating the program only on the basis of test scores
• Using standardized achievement tests as only one of many indicators of program outcomes	• Using standardized achievement tests as the only indicator of program outcomes (p. 191)

assessment instruments include (but are not restricted to) discussion, written tasks, journals, homework, special projects, and class presentations. "Simply put," states the *Standards,* "assessment should not rely on a single instrument or technique (p. 192)."

Standardized tests have long been a staple of American schools, but many educators know the downside of large-scale, norm-referenced tests. These tests don't always indicate the student's mathematical progress, reasoning ability, or conceptual understanding, but merely record the ability to provide the correct answer to a specific problem on a given day. Usually, standardized tests indicate what students do not know, rather than revealing what they do know. Placing undo emphasis on these tests leads administrators, parents, and the public at large to focus on the results of the assessment itself, when they could be focusing on the true understanding of the mathematical concepts the tests set out to evaluate.

It goes without saying, however, that there must be some form of accountability for instructional practice. Parents have the right to feel confident that their children are learning the concepts and facts that will enable them to succeed in the future; administrators must justify school procedures to parents and taxpayers; and teachers need to know that their methods of instruction are helping every child learn and grow mathematically. Many teachers are using methods, both formal and informal, that address these needs and at the same time more effectively assess the mathematical understanding of individual children.

INFORMAL ASSESSMENT

Informal assessment presents student progress in relation to the instructional content, often over time as students mature developmentally and progress mathematically. Informal assessment is characterized by its open-ended format and individualized nature, which allows it to be tailored to the needs of each teacher and each student. Perhaps best of all, this mode of assessment does not take time away from the instructional process. Rather, it can be incorporated into the math program, can benefit student instruction, and can help identify needed change in the instructional process.

There are many ways teachers informally evaluate students, for in a child-centered classroom almost everything a teacher does is aimed at knowing more about the students and what they are doing. Three specific methods, anecdotal records, student portfolios, and student journals, are representative of those that can be incorporated into mathematics programs at the primary-grade level.

Anecdotal Records

Teach-and-test methods of evaluation only assess percentages of correct (or incorrect) answers for a specific task, but anecdotal records provide a means to record student levels of thinking, reasoning, problem solving, and communicating mathematically. When compiled over time—a month, a year, or an entire elementary school career—they provide a lens through which to view student development and progress. When keeping anecdotal records, teachers are able to evaluate the concept development behind the answers, record which strategies seem to work best for a student, and pinpoint specific misconceptions that repeatedly interfere with conceptual understanding.

In classrooms where children are encouraged to construct their own understanding, every child is actively involved in math processes—investigating and acting on objects, describing those actions and results, sharing ideas with peers and adults, explaining thinking, and justifying solutions. Such classroom scenarios are rife with opportunities for teachers to observe, listen to, and record student thinking. Brief notes about student ideas, insights, and misconceptions provide glimpses of a child's thinking. As with portraits in a photo album, no one "picture" represents a child's total mathematical "history" and awareness. But when compiled over time, these pictures draw a more complete portrait of the child: her strengths, weaknesses, thinking style, and conceptual awareness—where she stands mathematically.

When children work in pairs or small groups, each child has a chance to participate actively and has a forum for discussion, negotiation, and the give and take of mathematical ideas common to group activity. Cooperative grouping facilitates anecdotal record keeping because it gives the teacher a chance to move about the room, observe student activity, and listen to each child. How else can she discover what each child is thinking?

Paired activity can be applied in almost any math situation. For example, when exploring the "favorite flavor graph," Ms. Howard might have begun by saying to the students, "Think about the graph for a minute. Now turn to the person next to you and tell that person something you noticed about the graph." With a single question, every child would be thinking, and then sharing, his or her ideas. At the same time, Ms. Howard would have had the opportunity to walk around the room and listen to the children's comments. Conversations that indicated specific misconceptions or good insight could have been recorded for notation in the child's record. The process could then have continued in the group discussion when many different ideas were explored.

Ms. Howard would not want to record every act or every comment she heard, but certainly some comments would stand out as unusual, and therefore important for her records. She might note that, like Jeffrey, several children seem to have a misunderstanding of patterns. The comments of other students might indicate an advanced concept development, perhaps an understanding of subtraction, or of subtraction facts.

Asking children to share one observation would pave the way for them to contribute one idea, but following this up by asking, "Who sees something different?" would prod the children to look at the situation from many new perspectives. This emphasis on different perspectives would have allowed Ms. Howard to assess the highest level of student thinking rather than the simplest and most obvious answers. Students must stretch their minds and use higher-level thinking skills to view a problem from many angles.

Teachers who make the rounds of the classroom while children are engaged in math activities, or who guide a whole group discussion in which children explain their thinking, are in the perfect position to make anecdotal records about each and every child in their class. This need not become a burdensome task. Few teachers make these notations all the time, even when something notable occurs. Rather, they designate specific activities as record-keeping opportunities—for example, those that involve students wrestling with a particularly important concept, such as place value.

Many teachers develop strategies that help them take notes more effectively and efficiently. For example, some teachers use "sticky" notes or labels as a quick way to record selective comments about student performance. Later they adhere them to student folders and then review them periodically to make sure no children are overlooked. Other teachers use loose-leaf notebooks with sections designated by student or subject and add pages as necessary. Many take advantage of instructional assistants, parent volunteers, or student teachers to take notes on students. However, because this deprives the teacher of direct observation, it might be more beneficial to have the assistant lead an activity while the teacher makes notes like those shown in Figure 8-1.

Figure 8–1 *Many teachers keep index cards with them as they observe and work with children. Separate cards can be filed under each child's name in a file box. It's fairly easy to update information on the cards.*

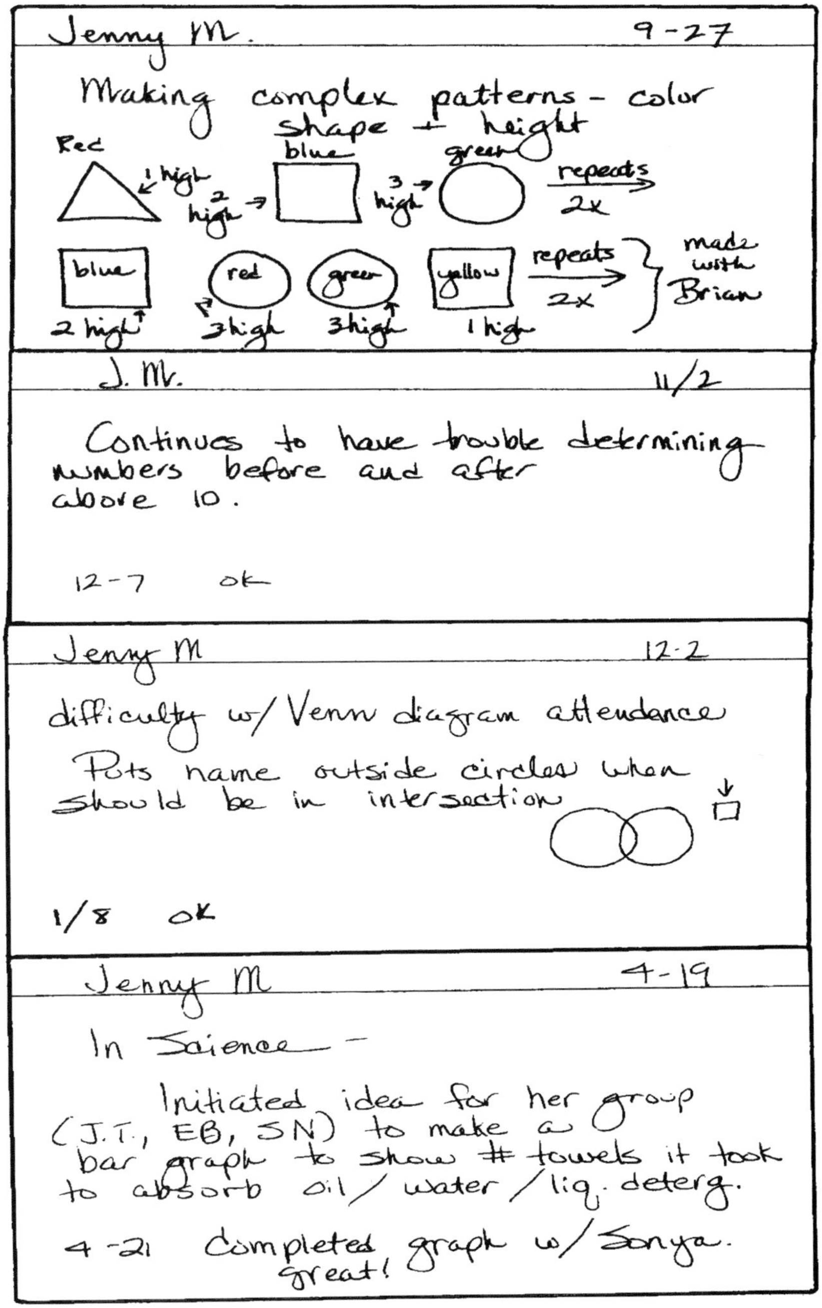

Portfolios

Mathematics portfolios provide a means to collect a representative sampling of student work over a period of time. They provide data with which to assess student's progress over the year, and to communicate that progress with parents, administrators, and the students themselves.

Because it is impractical to collect all student work, teachers must develop their own criteria for selecting the portfolio contents. For example, the teacher and the student can each choose one item to represent a week's work. Sometimes the teacher even encourages parents to choose a paper for their child's portfolio.

The child will probably decide to include the work she feels best about, and the parents, if they choose to contribute, will most likely pick a paper that they feel highlights the child's strengths. But there is some debate over which papers the teacher should choose. The general purpose of the portfolio is to show a sampling of work indicative of student achievement. But should the paper be the student's best work of that week, or work that is simply representative of her general performance? Obviously, this is the teacher's decision and must be based on his personal teaching philosophy and what he knows about his students.

However, there are strong arguments in favor of consistently including the best work from any student. No teacher will ever know with certainty that what he believes is typical of a child's performance actually represents what the child understands and can do. By consistently including a child's best work, he records what the child ultimately is capable of doing, and probably what she really understands. Additionally, a child's best work provides a basis for making appropriately challenging plans for upcoming instruction. In any case, whatever the decision, it should probably be noted in the portfolio.

At first glance, portfolio collections seem restricted to pencil-and-paper tasks. In fact, although their contents are limited to tangible forms, portfolios can include a variety of recorded materials. Photos can be taken of projects that cannot be included—group work, outdoor projects, a student-constructed bulletin board display. Students can create data collection records, narrative descriptions, pencil tracings, crayon rubbings, or illustrations of the hands-on activities and classroom experiences in which they were involved. What's more, besides providing a record for students' files, alternative recording activities have instructional benefit. Graphic representation, such as writing, drawing, or charting, provides closure and helps to concretize the abstract ideas children have after hands-on experiences.

Reviewing portfolios helps teachers document the mathematical progress of individual students and the class as a whole. But students, too, can benefit from their collected work when encouraged to review, assess, and reflect on their progress. Teachers can even create instructional activities that encourage personal reflection. An activity calling for personal reflection in math might incorporate writing, and integrate other subjects. For example, in May, second graders might look at a science measurement activity they did in September and compare it with one they did in February. What did they do differently in February than they did in September? Was it more efficient? What do they know now that they didn't even know in February? How would they teach that early September lesson to an incoming second grader next year?

Portfolios are student-specific assessment tools that document program content and student progress. When kept over the course of several grades, they indicate student strengths and development from year to year. Student portfolios provide a means of assessing where a student currently is in terms of his math understanding, how he is progressing, which modalities of communication appeal most to his individual strengths, and perhaps most telling, what he thinks is his best work.

The contents of one student's portfolio might include:

- an answer to an open-ended math question
- a description or photo of a group project
- an individual math project
- a math-related science project, such as collecting and recording weather data
- graphs done for social studies
- math-related work from another subject area
- story problems created by the student
- drawings done for math
- copies of interesting journal entries
- teacher anecdotes
- papers on which the student has corrected errors
- work done outside of school for math
- a math poster design

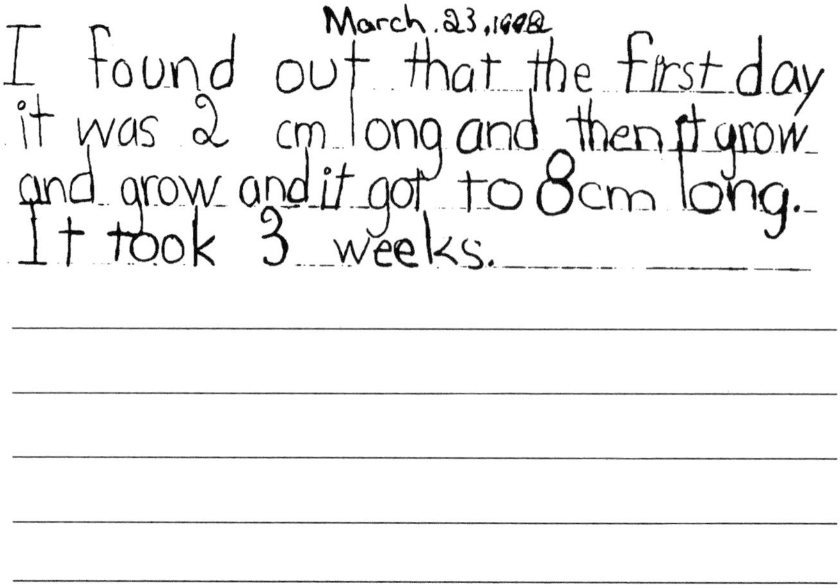

March 23, 1998

I found out that the first day it was 2 cm long and then it grow and grow and it got to 8cm long. It took 3 weeks.

Figure 8–2 *Journal writing allows children to record events, observations, and ideas.*

Student Journals

Student journals need not fall under the exclusive domain of the language arts curriculum. As many teachers are discovering, science, social studies, and even mathematics learning can benefit from personal reflection through journal writing.

Writing mathematical ideas serves much the same function as verbally discussing these ideas. It concretizes thinking. It helps forge connections among mathematics concepts. It demands that students break down abstract and intuitive conclusions into logical, sequential, and often replicable processes. And it allows students to do this in a nonrestrictive and nonjudgmental format. The journal is theirs. It is personal. They alone decide what they will write in it. Because children know that their entries will not be corrected, graded, or judged, they feel free to express their true thinking, not just the words they think the teacher will approve of. Consequently, journals like that shown in Figure 8-2, offer a window into students' understanding.

Mathematics journal writing in the primary grades can involve drawing pictures, writing equations, developing story problems, or discussing reactions to a math activity. Math journals can be graphic, numeric, or narrative. Usually, math journals at this grade level are responses to teacher-generated journal prompts. These can be tailored to demonstrate understanding of specific concepts the teacher is assessing, but should always be open ended. In kindergarten and first grade, class journals can be done using a language experience approach. The teacher can elicit (and assess) ideas from the children during a group discussion, and record those ideas on chart paper. The pages can be kept throughout the year on an easel, and/or copied into a smaller format for later reference.

Journal prompts (like those in Figure 8-3 on page 102) must be developmentally appropriate. The youngest children, those in kindergarten or just entering first grade, might be asked to draw a picture that shows six, or that illustrates what the children did during a mathematics activity. More mature students can be expected to use appropriate number symbols and narrative style. Prompts might require that students write five "number sentences" that use the number 10, or describe a sphere without drawing a picture. Or, students could be asked to respond to specific questions whose answers will provide special insight into their individual mathematical struggles, aptitudes, and attitudes.

When worded carefully, journal prompts can help a teacher assess the breadth of her students' grasp of a concept. For example, when trying to determine whether children view subtraction as more than just "take away," a teacher might carefully word a prompt asking students to write three story problems that use the equation $25 - 12 = 13$, and require that each story omit a different number of the equation. The resulting stories could indicate whether a child understands both comparative and missing addend subtraction.

Perhaps more clearly than any other assessment tool, student journals can serve the dual purposes of assessment and instruction. Joan Countryman, in her book *Writing to Learn Mathematics* (Heinemann, 1992), explains why writing helps mathematics learning: "Writing strengthens a student's experience of a new concept. Students get immediate feedback from the words that they produce. When students write, they are integrating the work of the hand, the eye, and the brain. They fix on the page connections and relationships between what they already know and what they are meeting for the first time (p. 10)." Later she explains why she values journal writing for her mathematics students: "Reading math journal entries tells me considerably more about what students grasp and do not understand, like and dislike, care about and reject as they study mathematics than any formal or traditional

Figure 8–3

Each prompt must be tailored to suit the needs of a specific teacher, group of students, and particular learning task. Some sample prompts taken from a variety of classes include:

- Show three different drawings for the number five (5).
- Write three story problems that have five (5) as an answer.
- Write about your favorite number. Tell why it is your favorite.
- Make up a pattern and tell about it.
- Find out how many windows are in your home. Tell how you did this.
- Write three story problems for the picture on page 45 of your book. Tell how to solve your problems.
- Find out the favorite ice cream flavor for ten people you know. Invent a way to show this information to our class.
- Spin this spinner ten times. Tell what happened. Tell why you think it happened.
- What was easiest for you in today's math lesson? Why?
- What was hardest for you in today's math lesson? Why?
- What did you like most in math this week? Why?
- Write ten problems that use the number 10.
- Try to solve these problems mentally (no paper, pencil, or calculator). Write how you solved them.
- Write how you would tell a younger child to do the work we learned in math today.
- Make up ten math problems that you think are easy to do without paper, pencil, or calculator. Tell why you think they are easy.

math assignments. I find myself more aware of what students know, and how they come to construct that knowledge (pp. 28–29)."

FORMAL ASSESSMENT

Using a variety of open-ended, informal assessment techniques gives a comprehensive picture of the instructional needs of individual students and the class as a whole. However, sometimes teachers, administrators, and parents feel more formal assessments are needed. Formal assessments can be described as any set of questions or tasks given to all students in a consistent and replicable manner. They do not necessarily have to result in a grade, but they do include evaluation of student mastery of specific concepts.

There are several reasons why teachers, or the school administration, may decide that formal assessments are worthwhile. Formal assessments can

- indicate whether the program is moving along in a consistent and productive manner
- provide an effective means to communicate with parents and administrators
- validate informal observations that the teacher has made about the students.

Sometimes, the results of the formal assessment are inconsistent with those of the informal assessments about a particular child. This suggests that the child's progress needs to be verified. Usually, it is the informal assessments that provide the most reliable data about a child's understanding. Inconsistencies in results might simply indicate that the child does not perform well in formal assessment situations.

Many school districts impose an array of formal assessment instruments on teachers and students. The classroom teacher often has little control over their inclusion in the school program. In such cases, a teacher could decide to supplement large-scale formal test results with results determined by assessment methods she has developed herself.

Student Interviews

Individual student interviews may or may not be considered formal testing. Though time consuming in a busy classroom environment, individual student interviews can provide sufficiently valuable information to justify the time involved. It is often beneficial for a teacher to meet with each student individually once, perhaps twice, during the year, to assess some aspects of mathematical progress. Such interviews aren't informal conversations, but rather a planned set of tasks that provide insight into a student's understanding of specific concepts. These interviews can be accomplished while the rest of the children are working independently.

If, for example, a teacher wanted to determine how well her students understood place value, she could develop an appropriate question, set out a variety of materials (base-ten blocks, multi-link cubes, or beans), and ask each child to solve the problem using any strategy he wanted. He could use the materials, draw a picture, or write the problem out numerically on paper, but he would need to explain what he did and why. By carefully designing four or five problems that address specific content areas, teachers can generate a picture of each student's mathematical development on that set of mathematical concepts. By requiring the same tasks of everyone, teachers can evaluate the progress of the class as a whole.

One set of questions for second graders might include the following prompts. Props for this task include four cards, one for each numeral— 1, 2, 3, and 4; and patterns for double-digit addition and subtraction (marked boxes to place each card).

Prompt One: Here are four digits on cards (1, 2, 3, 4). Here is a pattern for an addition problem. Arrange these cards on the pattern to make two double-digit numbers that, when added together, will equal the largest possible sum.

1.

Figure 8–4

Prompt Two: Here is a different pattern, this time for a subtraction problem. Use the cards to make a subtraction problem whose answer is the biggest possible number.

2.

Figure 8–5

These questions give insight into understandings of place value and operation. If a student responds correctly, he could go on to solve additional problems with different digits. If he answers incorrectly, then the follow-up might be for the student to simply arrange two or three of the digits to make the greatest number he can. If, after each response, students are asked to explain their thinking, some students may be able to correct their errors.

No single assessment method gives a total picture of a child's mathematical achievement or understanding. Each provides just a glimpse of the child at any one point in time. But like the combined pieces of a jigsaw puzzle, an array of assessments forms a reasonable, cohesive picture. When assessment instruments are teacher developed, they better evaluate specific students, present a clearer picture of the teacher's instructional strategies, and show the general progress of the teacher's mathematics program.

9

......

THE CASE OF ONE YOUNG
MATHEMATICIAN

*T*yrone *was handed the following card and was asked to solve the problem and explain his thinking.*

$$41 - 29 = \underline{\hspace{2cm}}$$

He proceeded with confidence. "First I should make this a 30," he said, pointing to the 29. "So I'll add one on. Later on I'll take it away. So you have 41 take away 30. That's 11, and then you take away the 1. That's 12."

What an interesting procedure! But as reasonable as it appears, it is a far cry from the traditional subtraction algorithm usually taught and required of children in the second grade. One wonders how successfully Tyrone would perform in a class that requires students to solve problems in the traditional manner. It is fortunate for Tyrone that since first grade, he has participated in a mathematics program that values student-created procedures and solutions.

Tyrone's nontraditional method of solving this subtraction problem did not obey the conventional rules taught for double-digit subtraction with regrouping. Yet it is a quick, efficient, and effective solution *for Tyrone*. It indicates an understanding of numbers and their relationships in the subtraction process. And it exemplifies the thought processes of a budding young mathematician.

Tyrone is a child with unusual math potential. He is thoughtful and highly verbal. His thinking is creative and unique, and demonstrates a well-developed insight into mathematical concepts. But Tyrone is very quiet, and despite his strong verbal capabilities and his obvious mathematical skills, he does not stand out in his class. In fact, because of his reserved manner, Tyrone could be passed over as simply another child of average ability. His uncommon approaches to solving math problems might even fool a teacher into believing Tyrone didn't grasp a concept. Add to this situation the fact that Tyrone attends a school that generally has low scores on standardized tests and therefore has low expectations placed upon its students, Tyrone's mathematical future might be bleak.

What if Tyrone were *not* in a math program that encouraged him to explain his thinking? He would be shown the traditional method of subtraction and would certainly have realized that it didn't match what he'd created. This could lead him to conclude that his method—or worse yet, his thinking—was wrong. He might even have difficulty understanding the traditional algorithm, for its logic is very different from his style of mathematical reasoning. What might this have done to his confidence? In any event, it is unlikely he would have had a chance to develop *his* style of thinking and reasoning, or emerge from the primary grades ready to think like a mathematician.

As with any mathematician, math is not always easy for Tyrone. Often he must wrestle with, and return to, a problem that he has difficulty solving, but his tenacity usually enables him to find a satisfying and creative solution. On one occasion, Tyrone was given the problem $42 - 25 = $ _____ . He wrote down 21 in the space provided, but seemed uncertain about his answer. Although he could have stopped at that point, he decided to try again. He copied the problem vertically, but placed the 25 above the 42.

$$\begin{array}{r} 25 \\ - \ 42 \\ \hline \end{array}$$

He subtracted the 2 from the 5 in the ones column and then stopped. He realized that he could not take the 4 from the 2.

Noting his perplexed look, his teacher asked whether he would like to use some base-ten blocks. Tyrone reached over and counted out four tens and two ones to represent the 42. To subtract the 25, he removed two of the tens and then counted up five places on one of the remaining tens. Using his finger to mark that spot, he counted what remained. "The answer is 17," he said, but with a tone of uncertainty.

He looked back at the paper and said "Let me look at this again." Then he rewrote the problem, this time placing the 42 on top, but got an answer of 23.

He noted that he now had three different answers: 21, 17, and 23. "Which one is right?" he asked.

The teacher turned it back to him. "Which do *you* think?"

"I think the blocks," he said hesitantly. "So I think the answer is 17."

The teacher had him write down his answer and she prepared to move on. But Tyrone was still not ready to let go. "Seventeen, plus twenty-five is. . . . What is seventeen plus twenty-five?" he asked aloud, as though still trying to remove his doubt. Without wasting a moment, Tyrone practically crawled across the table to grab the blocks back. He counted, this time taking a very sophisticated approach, "seventeen, twenty-seven, thirty-seven, thirty-eight, thirty-nine, forty, forty-one, forty-two. The answer was seventeen!" he said with certainty and great enthusiasm. And with the problem resolved, he was finally able to move on.

This was not a simple problem for a child Tyrone's age, and several times during this task the teacher gave him a chance to go on to the next problem. At least once, she started to pack up the materials, but Tyrone was not about to let this problem go unsolved. He had obtained three different answers. He knew this couldn't be, and he was obviously unsure of his paper-and-pencil arithmetic. Concrete materials gave Tyrone the means to discover the answer in a way he could see and understand, check his answer, and resolve the conflict left by the pencil-and-paper procedures.

At this point, Tyrone was ready to be encouraged to record the work he was doing with the base-ten blocks and make a direct connection between what he now believed to be a correct process and a pencil-and-paper record of it. That would give him an algorithm he understood. Later, he would be able to move to a more efficient (and perhaps traditional) algorithm if that proved useful to him.

It's highly probable that if Tyrone had been given similar problems on a worksheet, and not provided the time for reflection or the hands-on materials to support his work, he would have gotten many answers wrong. He would have learned nothing in the process; his teacher would not have seen his ability to stick with a problem or his capacity to solve it; and most importantly, he would not have gained the confidence that accompanies constructing a solution and then validating it. Tyrone would not have had the opportunity to connect his insightful work with blocks to a pencil-and-paper procedure.

Encouraging children to communicate their mathematical thinking reveals many student capabilities that would go unnoticed in a program that looks only for right or wrong answers. When children are given the tools and encouragement to convince *themselves* that they have gotten a correct solution, they gain an inner confidence that cannot be derived by having a teacher judge their work. Like Tyrone, they become mathematically empowered.

Sometimes Tyrone's explanations can be long and involved, and even confusing to the observer, but they usually indicate the complex understanding of mathematics that he is constructing for himself. When given the numbers 7, 5, 3, and 6 to add, Tyrone answered very quickly, "Twelve and nine is twenty-one." He had automatically broken the problem into two simpler addition problems, and then combined those answers to set up a new one.

"How did you know 12 plus 9 equals 21, Tyrone?" he was asked.

Interestingly, Tyrone's explanation does not even include the number 12. "Eleven plus nine is twenty because if you have a number [sic] like one and nine, you're going to have to get ten or one thousand or something like that. The number you get has to have a zero with it. So 11 plus 9 is 20. I took away that 1 from the 11. I added it back and it was 21." Though roundabout, Tyrone's procedure and subsequent explanation indicate a finely tuned number sense and growing understanding of the properties of addition.

On a later occasion, Tyrone was given this story problem: "Juanita has forty-six stickers in her sticker book. The book holds seventy-five stickers. How many more stickers can Juanita put in her book?" Without delay, he wrote the problem $75 - 46$ vertically and then figured the correct answer, 29.

When asked how he got 29, Tyrone began a very complicated answer that appears indicative of his "number sense." (One actually must read his explanation several times to fully grasp what he is saying.) "Twenty plus forty-six is sixty-six," he began. "Then I added a 9 plus the 20 and it was 29. Because 6 is more than 5." He pointed to the 6 in 46 and continued, "If this was a 5, then I would have picked 30 because 10 plus 5 is 15, so 9 plus 6 is 15. I needed to get the 5 right there and then I needed to get the whole answer." As in many of his other solutions, Tyrone found a way to work with a multiple of ten. He knew that 20 added to 46 would get him as close to 75 as possible without going over. If the problem involved 45 instead of 46, he explained, he could have added 30 to make 75. Quickly and intuitively he had devised a process to help him arrive at a solution.

Tyrone likes to count by tens. In a free moment between assessment tasks, he was overheard mumbling while pointing to a number chart. Asked what he was saying, he explained, "Oh, I'm just counting by tens," and proceeded to count, "Three, thirteen, twenty-three, thirty-three. . . ." Sheer mathematical enjoyment seems to provide an intrinsic motivation to explore numbers and their relationships.

When asked to count out seventeen chips one day, Tyrone got as far as, "One, two, three," and then stopped, smiled, and returned the chips to the pile. "I know a better way," he said. Moving the chips into five piles of three with two left over, he counted, "Three, six, nine, twelve, fifteen, sixteen, seventeen." His next task involved counting twenty-six chips. "Let's see how I can count. I'm going to count by fives." He arranged the chips in groups of five and counted them easily, "Five, ten, fifteen. . . ." After reaching twenty-six, he began to count the piles. "I was just wondering how many piles of five there are in twenty-five," he explained when he was done, then added, "There are five." As he so often does, Tyrone took this task not one, but several steps beyond what is called for. The reward for his ongoing investigation of number relationships is the continued discovery of more and more complex mathematics concepts.

With Tyrone, the enjoyment of mathematics is always evident, and there is little doubt that it is fundamental to his math development. Whether Tyrone's math appreciation and performance are the direct result of his school's mathematics program, or the manifestation of an innate mathematical aptitude is unimportant. The fact is, his talent and unorthodox procedures have not been squelched by rigid, rule-directed mathematics instruction. This has left him with the desire to explore mathematics and dig deeply into every experience.

What's more, his enjoyment seems infectious. At one point, a boy named Gerard joined Tyrone's class and the two became good friends. Neither Gerard's background nor his actions would have suggested he was a creative mathematical thinker. In fact, he appeared uninterested in school and unprepared to tackle mathematics problems that required higher-level thinking skills. But after several months in the class, Gerard showed indications of a growing mathematics awareness that went far beyond any initial impressions.

In one assessment, Gerard was given the numerals 1, 2, 3, and 4 on separate cards. He was then asked to arrange these cards to make two double-digit numbers that, when added together, would equal the largest possible sum. One natural tendency with this problem is to make the largest possible number first (43), and add to it the next largest number possible (21), making the problem 43 + 21. This is just what Gerard did. The teacher checked to make sure this was Gerard's final answer, gathered up the cards, and began to prepare the materials for the next problem.

"Wait a minute!" interrupted Gerard. He wanted the cards back. Quickly, he set them up to read 41 + 32.

"What made you change your mind?" asked the teacher.

"Well I kept thinking. Four tens plus three tens is more than four tens plus two tens," he said. "And I knew it didn't matter how the ones were." A few months earlier, no one saw or expected this kind of thinking from Gerard, but now Gerard was on the move with math.

Gerard's story underscores the value of giving children adequate time to reflect on their work, and opportunities to share with each other. Given a timed pencil-and-paper task that only focused on right and wrong answers, Gerard would have been marked wrong when he was actually quite capable of getting the right answer. Moreover, no one would have realized the sophisticated ideas that eventually led him to solve the problem correctly.

It's impossible to know how much Gerard was influenced by his friendship with Tyrone, but it is very probable that Tyrone is learning mathematics in a setting where he has the potential to powerfully influence others with his mathematical thinking and self-confidence. Undeniably, a mathematics program that encourages children to think creatively, to express that thinking, and to share cooperatively with their classmates, provides avenues of positive influence among its students.

Unfortunately, Gerard did not stay long in Tyrone's classroom. His family moved on to another school district, and he moved on to another math program. It is impossible to know what Gerard's future holds, or what influence his brief stay in this classroom will have on his mathematics development. It's also hard to know how many other Gerards sit in classrooms that do not spark an interest in mathematics, or how many Tyrones go unnoticed in programs that don't encourage creative thinking or support children's personal construction of understanding.

The capacity for creative mathematical thinking resides in virtually all young children, but it needs to be released and nurtured. This takes motivation, patience, and a mathematics program that is focused on the kinds of content and teaching approaches promoted by the NCTM *Standards*. "I don't care who tells me that Tyrone's ability to do math isn't something that this program created, that it's something that was in him all along," said one educator working with Tyrone. "I say to them, great! I'm glad that we didn't destroy it in him." Isn't this what all children deserve?

10

SOME QUESTIONS ANSWERED

We've seen how a child-centered program can help a student like Tyrone, but what about students who do not share his mathematical enthusiasm and interest?

All students learn when they are given the opportunity to construct their own understanding. Students who traditionally test low, those whose home and school backgrounds are not conducive to academic achievement, often flourish in programs that follow the NCTM *Standards*.

Eddie is a child whose academic performance is weak, his achievement low. His environment outside of school is not conducive to learning. Eddie tests poorly on questions that require rote memory. His problems are made even more difficult by the fact that he has not learned to read. In a recent one-on-one assessment, he appeared fatigued and complained that sirens had kept him awake the night before. Explaining a far-out answer he wrote on a pencil-and-paper problem, he said, "When I don't know something I just write down a number I haven't used in a long time." Without a doubt, Eddie is a student who would be headed for academic failure in a traditional system.

Fortunately for Eddie, his teacher encourages good thinking more than right answers, and has helped him to develop a mathematical sense. His understanding is strengthened and reinforced through teaching strategies that incorporate manipulative materials and student discussions, but his vocabulary is still weak and he often needs direct, one-to-one discussions with his teacher to aid his mathematics progress.

Recently, Eddie's teacher set up a unique geometry assessment, one designed to show analysis and reasoning skills rather than name recognition. In this activity, one pattern block was placed on the table and three others were tucked away in cloth bags. The children were asked to reach in the bags, feel each shape, and identify which shape matched the one on the table. Then they had to explain what attributes about the shapes led them to make their decision. This process encouraged the children to focus on the characteristics rather than the names of the shapes. Eddie did very well. He was able to use this tactile experience to identify the shapes and was guided in his discussion to explain his selection.

Had Eddie been asked simply to identify a rectangle or a triangle, he may or may not have given a right answer. In either case, he probably would have been guessing. He does not have the requisite vocabulary. But given the opportunity to focus on the attributes that made up the shapes and the relationships among these characteristics, Eddie was successful. Because he was thinking about the characteristics that are used to classify shapes, he was able to explain why one shape matched the rectangle and was not a parallelogram, or a circle, or a square. This is mathematics, not just rote memorization of facts and names, so in some ways, Eddie is ahead of his contemporaries, who are merely attaching names to visual cues.

It's clear that using manipulative materials will help the child who has difficulty understanding math concepts, but it can be time-consuming to use these methods for the whole class. Doesn't the fact that the students can complete the problems with pencil and paper indicate mastery of the concept?

In today's busy schools, it's easy to see why teachers might worry about the extra time it takes to incorporate hands-on strategies in math programs above kindergarten. However, allowing all children the opportunity to construct their understanding is never a waste of time. The underlying goal of any mathematics program in the primary grades should be to lay a strong foundation so that students will be prepared to meet the demands of later mathematics instruction and be able to relate mathematical ideas to real-world events.

Children can often complete arithmetic problems using traditional algorithms, but does this achievement on a pencil-and-paper test truly indicate mastery of a concept? Not always.

Jamal is a second grader who, in a pencil-and-paper assessment, correctly solved this double-digit addition problem with no regrouping:

$$\begin{array}{r} 72 \\ + 13 \\ \hline \end{array}$$

Later, he was given a similar problem, but this time he was asked to demonstrate the solution with base-ten blocks. He *constructed* the numbers correctly, using longs for the tens and single units for the ones, and it looked like he fully understood the process. However, when he went to name the number for the answer, he counted each block as one, regardless of whether it was a long or a single unit. This time, he reported the answer as 13. Jamal, it turns out, did not fully understand place value in the operation.

Jamal's incomplete understanding was masked by his pencil-and-paper work on a simple problem. He did not fully understand the concepts of double-digit addition and place value, and relied instead on rote memorization of rules. However, math without meaning does not withstand the test of time. Jamal may be able to pass through the early grades with ease, but unless he develops a more complete mathematical understanding, he will be lost when he encounters more complex mathematics.

Jamal's teacher decided that he needed to go back to the manipulatives and construct a stronger understanding. Then he'd be better able to translate that understanding into a paper record. She had him work directly with her and with a small group of students who had recently developed this understanding.

First, he worked with unifix cubes, counting out quantities, such as thirty-four or twenty-six. He was able to assemble sticks of ten and combine the sticks with single cubes to show how many tens and ones each number was. Then he moved on to solving some simple double-digit addition problems (with lesser numbers than are in the problem 72 + 13). Soon he was able to draw a connection between the cubes that could be assembled and the base-ten blocks that are already assembled. Finally, he was ready to reconsider problems like 72 + 13 with the base-ten blocks, and he successfully devised ways of recording on paper what he was doing with the blocks.

It is easy to assume student mastery when children perform well on pencil-and-paper tasks, but what about their ability to perform in real-world situations? Students need to see how the symbols on paper relate to real problems, real objects. They need multiple opportunities with problems and materials that help build mathematical understanding, and they need to record what they are doing with the materials so they can gradually develop the numeric skills that represent their work. Rather than being taught a teacher-generated algorithm, students need to construct their own procedures—procedures that have meaning to them and can be replicated and modified to meet the demands of more difficult mathematical tasks.

It's hard not to worry about children giving wrong answers and developing wrong procedures. Doesn't this reinforce misunderstandings?

In a program that focuses on building understanding rather than just giving right answers, teachers reinforce whatever right thinking brought the child to the correct or incorrect answer. As noted before, it's easier to value right thinking than a wrong answer, and this is more easily accomplished when teacher-generated questions lead to discussions rather than single answers.

Often, allowing a period of "wait time" provides the student with the opportunity needed to rethink the problem (as with Kevin in Chapter 7 and Gerard in Chapter 9) and establish a productive line of thinking. Some students may also need an example that relates to their problem or some manipulatives to model it.

When children are able to decide for themselves whether they are right or not, they will no longer need external verification from the teacher. They will gain confidence. They will believe that they can control the math rather than that the math controls them. Consequently, children will enjoy math and continue to strive towards greater math awareness.

This whole approach—just letting the children work with materials to build their own knowledge—sounds pretty laissez-faire. Where does the teaching come in?

The teacher's role in classrooms implementing the NCTM *Standards* is vital to student development. Students always need guidance from the teacher. While it's true that children must construct knowledge for themselves, it is the teacher who establishes what the goals for the mathematics program will be and how to help students move towards those goals. He will map out the plans for the year, design appropriate units, and develop meaningful situations for daily activities, always keeping in mind the fact that children construct understanding rather than absorb it.

The teacher maintains control of how the mathematics in each day's activity is developed. He places children in meaningful situations that require problem-solving skills. These might include manipulative materials, class-developed projects, or real-world situations, but each will incorporate circumstances in which children confront a problem and develop their own solutions.

Designing classroom situations is only the beginning of the teacher's role. He then must maximize an experience by developing its mathematics potential. Students need to make connections between their experiences and the math concepts. Student-student, teacher-student, and whole-group discussions help to bring out the mathematics. Teachers ask the questions that connect the experiences to the math and forge a link between previously acquired math concepts and those currently being addressed. It is these connections that build the knowledge structure necessary for a strong mathematics foundation.

Using manipulative materials without making these connections is not an effective instructional strategy, for if the bridge between the manipulatives and instructional math concepts is not built, students can wind up learning two procedures that they do not perceive as related—the manipulatives provide one procedure, the symbols become the other. If, for example, a teacher has his students subtracting with base-ten blocks, but never connects the block subtraction with subtraction using numeric symbols, he has created a burden for the children rather than a support. The children have memorized one set of rules for using the blocks and another set for using the symbols. Without guidance, they may never see the relationship.

The teacher's role in a *Standards*-based classroom cannot be overstated. It involves careful planning, which is then translated into well-organized activities. While students are participating in their activities, the teacher is moving about the class asking questions and offering support. He ensures that class discussions establish strong links between experience and concept, and he makes sure that these connections are being made by all children.

What are some hints for conducting productive class discussions?

It is not always easy to meet the needs of twenty-five students in a large-group discussion, and it is the skillful teacher, indeed, who is able to balance the needs of each student against those of an entire class.

However, many teachers have discovered certain guidelines that can help facilitate productive group discussions.

First, it is important to establish the goal of the group process. If the goal is only to hear correct answers, then the teacher need only call on the children raising their hands, listen to their answers, and move on to the next question. But in classrooms where the same students raise their hands all the time, the same students get called on all the time, and all the interaction between teacher and group is with those few students. The rest of the class remains passive and many students may not even participate mentally. The class may move on to new content, leaving many children still not understanding what has just been presented.

To help every child develop mathematical understanding and improve social and language skills, many teachers have decided to call initially on the quiet or reticent children. These children may need extra time and support to participate. They can be called on early in the discussion, before the more obvious ideas have been given, and allowed ample time to reflect and respond. (Using questions that have more than one answer encourages multiple responses from a group. See Figure 10-1 on the next page.)

When a student gives an answer, it is important to have him explain how he arrived at that answer. Correct answers might be the result of an intuitive flash or faulty reasoning. On the other hand, incorrect answers may represent only a minor error in an otherwise logical procedure. When children explain their thinking, teachers can uncover the logic behind the answer and students can clarify and confirm their own thinking.

Teachers often struggle with how to handle the student who gets stuck explaining an answer. Asking the child if she needs help, or even allowing her to call on a friend for assistance, sends the message that she is incapable of solving the problem herself. When the child feels that her teacher and classmates trust her to solve the problem and will allow her the time and support she needs, she is encouraged to try new ideas without fear of failure. Given time and confidence, she may develop a workable solution.

No matter how long the "wait time," however, some students simply will not be able to come up with an appropriate response. Possibly they lack sufficient background knowledge or are confused by some element of the problem. Maybe they need the freedom to think longer than the

Some Effective Inquiries

Tell me what you were thinking.

How did you get your answer?

How can you decide if it is right?

Does it seem to make sense? Why or why not?

Can you write a problem that is like it?

Can you act it out?

Can you show me a model of it?

Can you draw a picture of what happened?

Figure 10–1

group can afford. Chris Valentine confronted this situation when Danielle set out to explain her complicated grouping system, as described in Chapter 3. Realizing that Danielle needed more time, Chris moved on, returning to Danielle only when it appeared she was ready to continue. In situations in which it is less apparent that the student is ready or able to arrive at an answer or explain a solution, Chris returns to the student another day. She notes that these incidents often indicate specific weaknesses that need to be addressed through further classroom activities.

Many teachers believe that group discussions are essential to helping students clarify their thinking, establish mathematical procedures, and see math concepts from a variety of perspectives. They provide closure for almost any kind of classroom experience and offer teachers valuable means of assessing student learning.

Doesn't taking the time to have one child explain her thinking rob the rest of the students of time they need?

Not really. Harold Cutler, who taught an intermediate elementary grade, presented a number of problems to his class. "I want you to pick two problems that you can do in your head," he told them. "Be prepared to share your method."

The first child who raised her hand explained, "I picked 35 minus 21. I thought 5 minus 1 is 4 and 3 minus 2 is 1, so the answer is 14."

"Okay," said Mr. Cutler, "did anyone else do it a different way?"

"I said 35 minus 20 is 15 and 21 is 1 more than 20, so the answer must be 14," offered a second student.

"Did anyone do it a different way?" the teacher continued.

"I thought 35 is 5 times 7 and 21 is 3 times 7. I subtracted the 3 from the 5 and got 2, and 2 times 7 is 14," explained Brandy.

Although Brandy's unique approach involves mathematical procedures most elementary students would be unfamiliar with, it exemplifies the value of allowing the time for students to share their thinking. None of the other children, and few adults, would have thought of Brandy's unique method, but upon hearing her solution, some might think, "Maybe I can do that too."

Each individual approaches math problems in a slightly different way. Sharing these approaches not only concretizes procedures for the speaker, it broadens the possibilities for those listening. Tyrone, the young mathematician in Chapter 9, has a keen mathematical awareness. His own conceptual understanding is deep-rooted, but his approach is often unconventional. Although he is able to develop meaningful procedures for himself, he once told a teacher that he likes to hear his classmates' explanations because he often hears things he would not have thought of.

What about the children that just are not "good" at math?

Our schools, our teachers, and our students' parents need to foster the belief that *all* students can succeed in mathematics. Many people attribute the higher achievement of Japanese students to a greater natural mathematical ability. In reality, one factor in their mathematics achievement appears to be parental attitude. Japanese parents tend to feel that mathematics is a difficult subject, but with hard work any child can succeed. American parents, on the other hand, often feel that to succeed in mathematics, children need a natural ability or special talent (Stevenson, Lee, and Stigler 1986).

Allowing children the time and opportunity to construct their own mathematics understanding will help them develop a strong foundation. This, in turn, will assist them as they progress through more complex mathematics courses in future grades, regardless of what the initial perception of their "ability" may be.

Children who feel they are not good in math often have not been provided with enough opportunities to experience success. They may not have been presented situations in which they could connect their personal experiences to school mathematics. Virtually all children functioning in our school systems have the ability to achieve mathematically in their own time and in their own way. It is the teacher's mission to help each child realize her math potential through successful completion of activities at her own level, free of stress and anxiety.

"Math anxiety" just seems a part of our culture. How can we keep it from affecting our students?

Many teachers themselves feel anxious about mathematics. Teacher math anxiety and student math anxiety are related; if a teacher feels anxious about math, she is probably going to communicate this to her students. Math anxiety probably originates from the kind of mathematics program so many teachers experienced as students themselves—a program that emphasized getting the right answer and using rules provided by the teacher.

Jannelle Riviera has taught in primary grades for seventeen years. She chose early childhood education, she admits, because of her anxieties about math and science. She was fairly sure she could handle the first-, second-, and even the third-grade curricular content, but did not feel capable of teaching more difficult concepts. Once she began teaching, she restricted her mathematics program to "math time" and never veered from the prescribed path. Then her school joined a project that helped teachers implement an NCTM *Standards*-based program. She knew it was time to rethink her attitudes towards mathematics. She was surprised by the results.

Rather than being the burden she'd expected, Ms. Riviera has found that following the program actually provides relief from her long-standing anxiety; that is, when she allows her students the time and opportunity to construct their own mathematics knowledge, the pressure is off. She now sees her responsibility as placing children in situations in which they can work individually or together to solve problems that will move them towards the intended math concepts.

"I don't have to have all the answers," she explains. "I need to provide a situation where the kids are going to be motivated to explore

Allowing children the time and opportunity to construct their own mathematics understanding will help them develop a strong foundation.

and discover. Sometimes it's difficult to accept that you don't have to have all the answers, but the fact is, even when you do, you should restrain yourself from giving solutions. Students need to discover these for themselves."

It is always easier to know the general math concept and the specific, final solution before presenting a problem to the class. In that way, if and when children get stuck, you can guide them in the right direction. But this is not essential. Teachers who do not know an answer can freely admit this to the students. Saying things like, "Let's see if we can work it out together," or "Maybe there's another teacher in the school who can help us," shows students that everybody has to work at finding solutions at some time.

How can I help students solve story problems?

For years children were taught to look for "clues" or "key words" in story problems. These were words that told them whether they needed to add, subtract, multiply, or divide. And in the neat world of textbook math, problems were always written to follow these specific rules. However, real-life problems do not work this way, so students need to develop the means to understand both the problems and the math within the problems to find appropriate solutions. There simply is no magic formula for solving problems, and asking children to rely on universal rules discourages them from thinking about mathematics problems.

One classroom displayed a wall chart labeled, "Clue Words for Story Problems." Listed on the chart were a series of "clues" and their meanings, including, *all together* means . . . *add*. Although that frequently is the case, the real world does not usually come equipped with clue words. What happens when a child who relies on this chart encounters a problem like the following: Terri collects trading cards. For her birthday, Daniel gave her twelve cards. Now she has forty-five altogether. How many cards did Terri have before her birthday?

The best mathematicians use a variety of techniques to help them understand and solve problems. Children, too, need to develop a repertoire of strategies and techniques that will work for them. Teachers can use ideas similar to those presented in the reading curriculum when promoting critical-thinking skills in their students.

In reading instruction, children are often taught dramatization, visualization, and prediction strategies to assist their comprehension.

Whether the goal is reading comprehension or mathematical problem solving, dramatization helps children understand the characters and events in that story. Consequently, the story takes on more meaning for the reader. Similarly, manipulating concrete materials that represent story components allows children to model situations and better understand problems. Visualization techniques also help concretize story ideas. Students can organize their thoughts graphically by making a web, matrix, drawing, or time line. Prediction helps develop a context for reading and similarly, in math, the use of prediction (sometimes in the form of estimation), provides a basis for finding logical solutions or judging a solution's reasonableness once it is found.

Sometimes the best problem solvers are those who take full ownership of a story problem. Teachers can make stories meaningful for children by incorporating events and ideas that students can value and identify with. In turn, these problems become inherently interesting and encourage students to seek solutions. Having students write problems for each other can increase the level of ownership as well as interest.

Enrico, a second grader, was completely distracted as he waited to begin an oral math assessment at school. He spent his time alternately sliding under his chair and climbing on top of his desk. He gave every indication that he was not listening.

"Tiffany has three snakes . . ." began the teacher.

"Snakes!" interrupted Enrico. "SNAKES!" He was delighted to hear a question about his favorite creatures and to discover that his classmate Tiffany had a collection of them.

His teacher continued, "Malcolm has some snakes too."

"Malcolm! MALCOLM!" Enrico interrupted again. "He's my best friend."

Enrico's body language suggested that he was not paying attention to the task at hand. In a more traditional setting, his teacher might have been tempted to reprimand him for being disruptive. But this teacher realized that Enrico's energy could be focused when learning situations are made meaningful.

Enrico is a child who really brings life to math stories. This problem became real to him because he could associate with his friends Tiffany and Malcolm and value their collection of snakes. Enrico went on to solve the problem and was ready for another.

Some children actually alter stories to create personal meaning. Nikki, a kindergartner, was asked, "If you have twelve cupcakes and want to share them with two friends, how many cupcakes will each child have?" Before she answered, she was asked to restate the question. "Well," Nikki began, "I have twelve cupcakes and I want to have a party. I ask Jessie and Amanda to come to my party . . ." She reconstructed the story to suit her own needs and then solved it. Many children have difficulty with this type of problem because they can't decide whether they should be counted in the group sharing the cupcakes. Rethinking the problem as a personal experience is one way to avoid this error.

Nikki is used to personalizing story problems. Her teacher encourages her students to create meaning from the story problems in their textbooks. In pairs, students read different story problems and decide how they can communicate their problem to the rest of the class. They might retell it in their own words, dramatize it, or model it with concrete objects. Then they describe how they would determine the solution.

Isn't it better to have children grouped by ability?

Often, teachers do not have any control over the students assigned to their particular class. Some schools evenly distribute students across classrooms; others assign teachers more homogeneous groupings. Whatever the case, there is usually a range of ability and achievement within a class, and with it comes the opportunity to incorporate both homogeneous and heterogenous in-class groupings. Fluidity of grouping allows teachers to change group assignments weekly, by subject, or with each activity.

There is no clear evidence that ability grouping improves learning, even for highly able students. In fact, there is evidence that ability grouping can have a negative effect on average- and low-achieving students. There may be indications that the highly gifted benefit from ability grouping, but even these results are mixed. Evidence of long-term differences seems especially difficult to find. (Secada 1992, 650–652.)

Furthermore, achievement levels in the early grades do not always reflect the ability to learn, but rather, indicate enriched early childhood experiences or differing levels and rates of maturity. Heterogeneous grouping in the primary grades helps to keep opportunities of advancement equitable while children mature and build a common history of experience. See Figures 10-2, 10-3, 10-4, 10-5, and 10-6 on the following pages.

Figure 10–2 *Assignments that allow children to make choices and seek their own level of comfort are particularly useful in heterogenous groups. Here, second-grade students were provided with a set of items they could "purchase" at the prices indicated, and then asked to write story problems. Each child completed the assignment at his or her own level of understanding.*

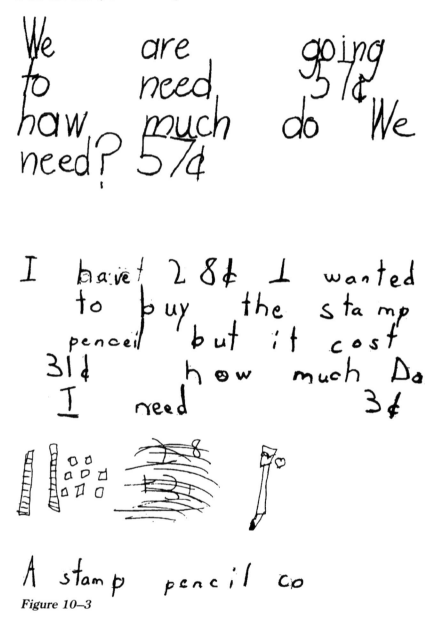

We are going to need 57¢
how much do We
need? 57¢

I have 28¢ I wanted
to buy the stamp
pencil but it cost
31¢ how much Do
I need 3¢

A stamp pencil co

Figure 10–3

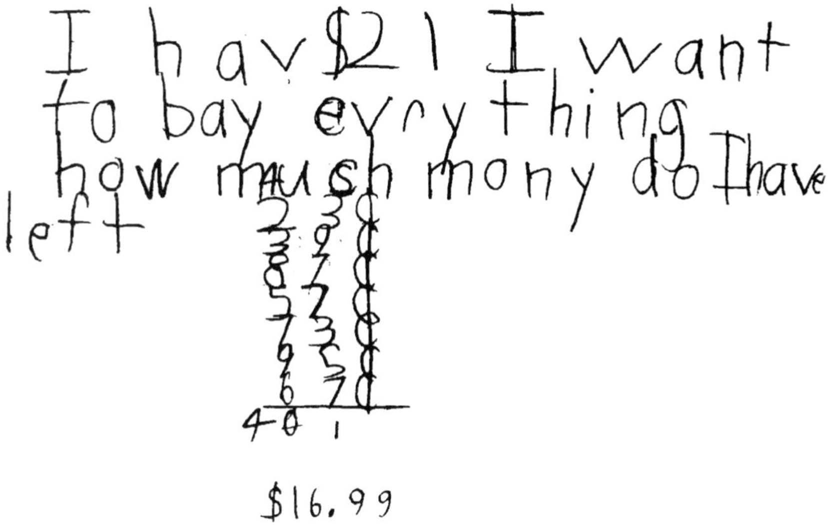

I have $21 I I want
to bay eyrything
how mush mony do I have
left

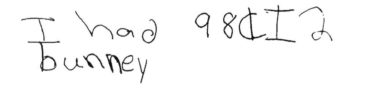

$16.99

Figure 10–4

I had 98¢ I 2
bunney

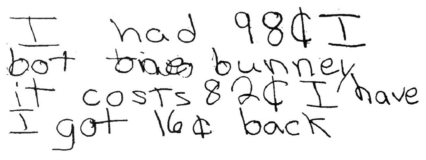

I had 98¢ I
bot bine bunney
it costs 82¢ I have
I got 16¢ back

Figure 10–5

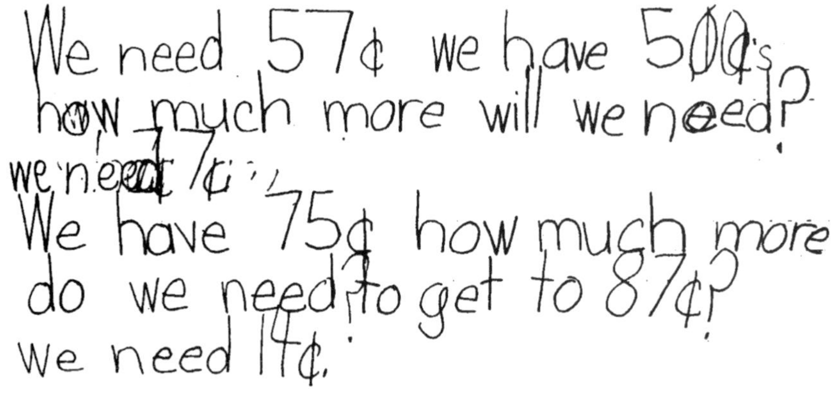

We need 57¢ we have 50¢'s
how much more will we need?
we need 7¢
We have 75¢ how much more
do we need to get to 87¢?
We need 11¢.

Figure 10–6

Despite fears to the contrary, heterogenous grouping rarely holds back the more able students. In fact, moving very bright children ahead through the curriculum until they reach the point at which they get frustrated serves no purpose, especially in elementary grades. When children are rushed quickly into the abstract, they often encounter a very narrow channel of instruction. At some point in the future, they will need to look at ideas from a variety of perspectives, and if they haven't had the opportunity to do that in elementary school, they could face serious trouble when required to do it in later years.

In groups where children work together cooperatively, students learn from each other. Heterogeneous groups offer a real mix of ideas, strengths, talents, and learning and reporting styles. Few children are unable to contribute something to the group process in a cooperative learning situation. Those who are slower at reading or writing are often very verbal. Children who intuitively reach solutions can learn from those who develop procedures step by step.

Tyrone, the highly able math student so often discussed in this text, is a product of frequent heterogeneous group experiences. His role in any mixed group would undoubtedly benefit the other children. He is able to articulate math processes, explaining and justifying each step along the way. But the benefits of mixed ability grouping are hardly one-sided. Rather than holding him back, Tyrone's group experiences enrich him. He enjoys listening to other children explain how they did things in ways that he would never have thought of. Even though Tyrone is very able, there are always ways to approach a problem that he hasn't yet considered.

In those activities in which the content is highly sequenced, the benefits of homogeneous grouping may equal or outweigh the drawbacks. Children who have strong backgrounds and are ready to move on to more complex concepts can push each other ahead, and those who are less advanced in the sequence will not be confused or frustrated. For example, in a unit on fractions, it may be wise to occasionally group together those children who are ready to handle symbolic representation if and when the need to work with symbols arises. Grouping them with children who are not yet ready for the complex structure of fraction symbols could create problems for both sets of students.

Some educators believe, however, that with carefully crafted instructional planning, these problems can be minimized or avoided. For example, the teacher can assign a heterogeneous group a variety of tasks that require different levels of skill and/or concept development. The teacher can encourage the group to let each child work on a manageable portion of the overall task and have the total group share responsibility for the completed *set* of tasks.

Some of this could take place at home. An older sibling, parent, or caregiver could ask a child to cut one slice of bread into two fair shares, another into four fair shares, and a third into six fair shares. Then, with the older person's help, the child could record likenesses and differences among the various fair shares. This assignment would provide a learning opportunity for children who are able to use symbolic representation, while those who haven't yet acquired that facility could describe the comparisons in words. The teacher can suggest in a note to parents the kinds of comparisons children can be guided to discover.

What about homework?

Homework can play an important role in the math program. When approached constructively, it helps students to think about mathematics outside of the classroom and gets parents involved in their children's education.

Often the biggest problem with homework arises from parents who expect to see their children bring home the same kind of math homework they did when they were in school. However, drill-and-practice worksheets or textbook assignments rarely contribute to mathematics awareness outside of school.

Parents need to know what the mathematics program is about so that they will understand the types of homework assigned. Early in the school year, teachers can explain in a letter to parents what they should expect their children to be doing for homework, and why the teacher believes in these assignments. This is also a good opportunity to let parents know how they can help their children progress mathematically, what types of home experiences to offer, and what types of questions to ask their children.

More and more schools are holding "family math programs" in the evenings. These family nights serve several purposes. They convey the message that mathematics is important, and they provide teachers and administrators an opportunity to explain the new views in math education and why school and home assignments may not look like those the parents have experienced. They also offer a format that allows teachers to model for parents various ways to interact with children when they do math homework.

Computational homework, done within the context of a meaningful activity, might involve other curricular areas or reinforce content being covered in school. Students might write a story that incorporates math concepts. They might count or measure the doors in their home or graph the number of rooms. They could even take a math game home from school and teach it to the family, or they could develop a game at home to bring to school. Parents and students can work as partners in activities and then discuss and record together what they have done.

What about using calculators and computers in the classroom?

Calculators and computers are part of the real world and are here to stay. They take away the drudgery of mathematics, improve efficiency, and increase accuracy of computation.

Many times children are handed pages of drill-and-practice problems to compute. The students complete them, check them, and correct them, only to be handed more of the same, even when they have done the initial work correctly. "Why should we spend thousands of dollars to teach children to do poorly what a five-dollar machine can do well?" asked Judah Schwarz in a presentation to the NCTM in 1989.

The NCTM *Standards* states that "the K–4 curriculum should make appropriate and ongoing use of calculators and computers (p. 19). " The value of technology in the K–4 classroom is frequently overlooked and too often relegated to filling a gap in unstructured "free-time" activity. It can, however, play an integral role in the mathematics curriculum.

To ensure that computers and calculators are used in a constructive manner, which is to complement or enhance mathematics, teachers can take specific steps to introduce these tools and provide for their independent use. The *Standards* advises that to use these tools effectively, "educators must develop a broader view of the various ways computation can be carried out and must place less emphasis on complex paper-and-pencil computation (p. 19)."

Calculators are instructional tools as well as devices to improve computational efficiency. Students can use calculators to investigate number patterns and the effect of computational algorithms. Such investigations would often be impossible without the calculator. Used this way, calculators provide a dimension to the instructional program that could not be achieved with pencil and paper alone.

Teachers can use computers with a whole class or for independent student work. One of the difficulties in using computers is the time required for the teacher to review and determine appropriate uses for the software; but working together and sharing ideas and experiences, teachers can share information about software within and between schools, so that the time required of any individual teacher is minimized.

If the number of computers is limited, then small-group or whole-class use is probably necessary. Much of the software that is intended for individual use can be adapted to whole-class instruction. Groups can view problems on a large screen while individual students take turns operating the keyboard. The students can work in pairs to decide on a response, and the group can decide on the entry through a class discussion.

It must be noted that when children are constructing knowledge, hands-on work is the primary class activity, and the computer medium does not lend itself easily to such activity. Additionally, many believe that relatively little in the way of quality software appropriate for the primary grades exists.

Students need to see classroom technology as tools that help them understand math better and extend their problem-solving capabilities, rather than as devices that excuse them from doing math. The potential exists for children to think that they should automatically use the computer or calculator whenever they are allowed, but they should learn that it is sometimes more efficient to use other methods—mental math, pencil and paper, or perhaps estimation—when they don't need an exact answer. In classrooms where students are asked to explain their thinking, they can also explain how and why they used a calculator, and then justify that decision, just as they would explain and justify any problem-solving technique.

In a nutshell, what are the most important things I can do to implement the *Standards* in my classroom?

1. Provide meaningful situations in which children can solve problems through the use of manipulative materials, interesting activities, and real-life situations.
2. Provide ample time for children to construct their own knowledge, reflect on their activities, and exchange ideas with peers and interested adults.
3. Encourage children to explain their thinking and how they arrived at a solution. Support their methods and ideas through thoughtful questioning. Make it a priority to have students rely on themselves to solve mathematics problems, *to be mathematicians*. The goal is, after all, math power for all students.

How can I get a copy of the NCTM *Standards?*
Write or call:
National Council of Teachers of Mathematics
1906 Association Drive
Reston, VA 22091-1953.
Information: (703) 620-9840
Orders: (800) 235-7566

WORKS CITED

Carpenter, T.P., and J.M. Moser. 1984. "The Acquisition of Addition and Subtraction Concepts in Grades One Through Three." *Journal of Research in Mathematics Education* 15: 179–202.

Countryman, Joan. 1992. *Writing to Learn Mathematics*. Portsmouth, NH: Heinemann.

Fuson, K.C. 1986. "Teaching Children to Subtract by Counting Up." *Journal for Research in Mathematics Education* 17: 172–89.

Irons, Calvin, and Paul Trafton. 1992. *Moving into Math*. Grade 1. San Francisco: MIMOSA.

National Council of Teachers of Mathematics. 1989. *Curriculum and Evaluation Standards for School Mathematics*. Reston, VA: NCTM.

National Council of Teachers of Mathematics. 1990. *Professional Standards for Teaching Mathematics*. Reston, VA: NCTM.

National Commission on Excellence in Education. 1983. *A Nation at Risk: The Imperative for Educational Reform*. Washington, D.C.: U.S. Government Printing Office.

National Science Board Commission on Precollege Education in Mathematics, Science, and Technology. 1983. *Educating Americans for the Twenty-first Century: A Plan of Action for Improving the Mathematics, Science and Technology Education for All American Elementary and Secondary Students So That Their Achievement Is the Best in the World by 1995*. Washington, D.C.: National Science Foundation.

Secada, W.G. "Race, Ethnicity, Social Class, Language, and Achievement in Mathematics." In *Handbook of Research on Mathematics Teaching and Learning*, edited by D.A. Grouws. 1992. New York: Macmillan Co.

Stevenson, H.W., S.Y. Lee, and J. Stigler. 1986. "Mathematics

Achievement of Chinese, Japanese, and American Children." *Science* 231: 693–99.

Thornton, C.A., and P.J. Smith. 1988. "Action Research: Strategies for Learning Subtraction Facts." *Arithmetic Teacher* 35 (no. 8): 8–12.

Whiten, David J., Heidi Mills, and Timothy O'Keefe. 1990. *Living and Learning Mathematics: Stories and Strategies for Supporting Mathematical Literacy.* Portsmouth, N.H.: Heinemann.